Partnerships in Math Education

The Power of University–School Collaboration

Chris Ohana

HEINEMANN
Portsmouth, NH

Heinemann
A division of Reed Elsevier Inc.
361 Hanover Street
Portsmouth, NH 03801-3912
www.heinemann.com

Offices and agents throughout the world

© 2003 by Chris Ohana

Library of Congress Cataloging-in-Publication Data
Ohana, Chris.
    Partnerships in math education : The Power of University–School
Collaboration / Chris Ohana.
        p. cm.
    Includes bibliographical references.
    ISBN 0-325-00297-5 (acid-free paper)
    1. Mathematics—Study and teaching (Elementary)—Texas—Case
studies. 2. Teachers—Training of—Texas—Case studies. I. Title.

QA135.6 .O36 2003
372.7'09764—dc21

                                                                2002192223

Editor: Victoria Merecki
Consulting editor: Susan Ohanian
Production editor: Sonja S. Chapman
Cover design: Joni Doherty
Compositor: Publishers' Design and Production Services, Inc.
Manufacturing: Steve Bernier

Printed in the United States of America on acid-free paper
07 06 05 04 03 DA 1 2 3 4 5

Contents

....

Acknowledgments

I enjoyed the company of many accomplices in the development of this book. First, the teachers of Lincoln and Forest provided help, encouragement, and inspiration to me in the years of the project. I thank them for their dedication to their students and the students of Midwestern. Second, Ann Thompson and Janet Sharp provided extended years of support and prodding as I wrote this book. I am deeply indebted to them for their goodwill and patience.

My family could not quite believe this project would ever end. And yet when I began to harbor doubts, they sacrificed time and, if necessary, gave me a swift kick. "The book" is now done, and I cannot imagine it could have happened without them.

1

The Collaboration

It was the start of the 1996–1997 school year and I was in a new job. It was my dream job—teaching science at Lincoln Elementary, a science magnet school. I had two beautiful laboratories and all the resources I could ask for. Just as I was starting to get a sense of my schedule and the school climate I was asked to attend a meeting with my principal, Grace Jordon, and some faculty members from nearby Midwestern State University (MSU)—"about math," Grace said.

The meeting was held at Lincoln. I arrived earlier than everyone else and sat in the meeting room, officially a parent/community center. I took stock of the room. It was cozy, with couches, kids' toys, and a few older computers along one wall. It was my first time in this room. Over the next few years I would come to memorize this place, the scene of meeting after meeting.

The others arrived simultaneously, as if they had all just come from another meeting. Grace, escorted two MSU faculty members into the room. As a former employee and current graduate student at MSU, I knew both of them. I knew Amy Roberts, the chair of MSU's Department of Curriculum and Instruction, best. I had traveled with her to science meetings around the country. The other was Karen Black, an untenured assistant professor. We knew each other in passing, but I knew little more about Karen than that she taught mathematics methods. Karen and I had little idea how much that meeting would change our professional lives in the next four years. It marked the beginning of a major event in the history of Lincoln Elementary and MSU, and for the university faculty member who directed the project we began to plan that day, the Mathematics Is Everywhere collaboration.

Our goals for the project were not modest. We sought to fashion a university–school partnership to improve mathematics teaching, a partnership in which elementary schools and universities would learn from each other. We planned that through the program,

- Inservice teachers would become active partners in preservice education by mentoring university students and teaching in the preservice program.
- Inservice teachers would have the opportunity to participate in professional development activities of their own design and choosing.
- Preservice teachers would learn in a mathematically rich university program, with classes that emphasized the integration and importance of mathematical concepts.
- A cohort of preservice teachers would observe and participate in the elementary schools as they applied their growing knowledge of teaching and content.
- University faculty would extend or rejuvenate their understanding of teaching and learning in the elementary classroom.
- University faculty would incorporate the experience and knowledge of practicing teachers in their courses.
- Faculty would join with elementary school teachers in collaborative, classroom-based research.

In this Camelot of mathematics reform, we attempted to blur the boundaries between higher education and the elementary classroom.

The Partners

In addition to primary-grade teachers from Lincoln, the collaboration would also include teachers from Forest Elementary, which serves grades 3–5. Lincoln and Forest were paired as a tool for desegregation in the 1970s. Their many years of history together led many in the community to refer to them as a single, hyphenated entity: Lincoln-Forest. In fact, on my first visit to Lincoln, I drove to Forest, thinking it was one school. Both schools have undergone a series of metamorphoses in their lives as magnet schools, in the ten years before the MIE project began settling into a focus on science. Despite being magnet schools, Lincoln and Forest weren't able to attract students from outside their attendance areas. It was difficult to entice families to bus their young children across town to what was perceived as a dangerous neighborhood, just for a little extra science instruction. Ninety percent of students lived in the immediate neighborhoods.

Lincoln, built in the early '70s, is located in a neighborhood of old Victorian-style homes. Some houses are vacant, boarded up, and decaying, while others have been maintained with care. The neighborhood is a high-crime, low-income area. It has a large African American population in a city and state that are more likely to claim a Scandinavian heritage. The principal at Lincoln, Grace Jordon, was a proud neighborhood resident who fiercely defended the neighborhood and its children. Lincoln had about 300 students in the open-classroom building. Slightly more than half of the students lived in the neighborhood. The others arrived in buses from the Forest area. Lincoln's physical appearance is striking. It has a huge playground with a large garden. In the year our project began, the entry had science, mathematics, and technology murals on each wall. On the way to the office, visitors passed an indoor pond with large, ornate fish. You couldn't help but hear the birds in the walk-in aviary to the left, in front of two science laboratories. Each lab had kid-size lab benches, sinks, and storage cabinets. Behind the labs were the kitchen used by classes and the photography darkroom. It's hard to imagine that any other K–2 building in the country, public or private, could have been as grand.

Forest is located in a stately tree-lined neighborhood with many brick Tudor-style homes. Residents are largely middle- or upper-middle class and white, though the area is more integrated than many other neighborhoods in the city. While the Lincoln and Forest areas are adjoining, a prominent private university effectively separates them. In contrast to Lincoln, Forest has a distinctly traditional look about it. An old three-story brick building, it housed about 250 students at the time. Built in different phases, the school is a challenge to negotiate. Some floors are inaccessible from certain stairwells. Small rooms are tucked away in various recesses formed by mismatching flights of stairs. The interior walls are painted a drab, institutional green. The floor tiles are cold and uninspiring. Except for a stairwell mural and a third-floor science classroom, the school's science focus wasn't obvious that year. But despite the institutional look of the hallways, some of the spacious classrooms in the older parts of the building border on the spectacular, with elegant woodwork and bay windows. The art room has beautiful cabinets, hardwood floors, and a panoramic view of the neighborhood. You can't judge Forest by its hallways—you have to get into its classrooms.

At the time the MIE project began, the differences between the schools' neighborhoods and physical characteristics paralleled a deep rift between their staffs. The schools had shared a single principal until 1994, but the challenge of uniting the staffs, which had distinctly different cultures, proved overwhelming. The Lincoln staff was generally much younger. The Forest staff was older and, if one listened to Lincoln teachers, more traditional. Lincoln teachers ached when they sent their little eight-year-olds on to third grade because they saw Forest as a harsh, impersonal institution. According to the Forest staff, the Lincoln teachers were nonchalant and naive. They scratched curious slang remarks on children's folders and failed to teach the children discipline. The relationship between the schools was a curious marriage.

The third MIE partner was Midwestern State University, a large land-grant university located in a rural county forty miles north of the city. Its College of Education enrolled more than 800 elementary education majors at the time. Although it didn't participate in the Holmes Group or the Goodlad consortium, two prominent higher education reform efforts, certain faculty members took notice of the changes recommended by those groups, which included improved academic preparation of preservice teachers; closer ties between university students and faculty and area elementary schools; and a renewed commitment to the democratic purposes of education. In response, MSU developed a small experimental program in 1990 that became known as Learning in Context (LiC). LiC was designed to increase the connections between preservice teachers at MSU and area elementary schools, increase the ties between MSU faculty and the schools, and offer education students courses in democracy and education. Thirty undergraduates were admitted into a LiC cohort each year. The students in a cohort took all of their education courses together and participated in extended field experiences in partner schools. Cohort 5, the undergraduates in LiC's fifth year, were placed at Lincoln-Forest.

Lincoln-Forest and MSU were not strangers to each other. The Mathematics Is Everywhere project grew out of a relationship that spanned two decades. In fact, MSU was involved with the initial

4

preparations to make Lincoln and Forest science magnet schools. When the district made the decision in the early 1980s that the schools would focus on science, an MSU professor conducted a series of science workshops for Lincoln-Forest teachers. In more recent years, an annual statewide Eisenhower workshop (a federally funded math and science professional development program) took place at Lincoln, with spaces reserved for a team of teachers and administrators representing Lincoln and Forest. Through the Eisenhower grant, Lincoln annually hosted a free summer session in mathematics and science for neighborhood children. MSU provided preservice teachers to staff the summer classes, and provided a supervisor for them, thereby giving its undergraduates valuable inner-city teaching experience. That experience extended into the following school year as MSU practicum students enrolled in science and mathematics methods ran an after-school science club for children at both Lincoln and Forest. This project ran until the retirement of the university professor in 2000.

Lincoln and Forest also provided several opportunities for MSU students to participate in special student-teaching assignments and field experiences. A few MSU student teachers had an extended stay (sixteen weeks) in one grade level. Their assignments required them to work with social service agencies that served Lincoln-Forest families. This program was wildly popular with Lincoln-Forest teachers, who valued the extended experiences with the student teachers—many so highly that they would no longer entertain the idea of a traditional eight-week student teacher placement.

Although there was a preexisting relationship between the two elementary schools and the university before the MIE project began, it was largely a case of "playing alone together." The schools gained by having free labor to run the summer school and the after-school science and math club. The preservice teachers benefited from the summer workshop. The university profited from being able to offer a summer experience to preservice students and from having a state-of-the-art facility for workshops. Despite the mutual benefits, however, there was no systematic or sustained interaction between the university and the schools. After the two-week Eisenhower summer workshop, university faculty disappeared from the schools, and Lincoln-Forest teachers had no occasion to travel to the university. MSU and Lincoln-

Forest shared in each other's bounty without forging any deep connections.

The Leaders

Many people from both schools and the university had a hand in developing MIE, but the project's leadership was a smaller group. Because MSU initiated MIE and had the job of pursuing fundable projects, the university took the lead.

Amy Roberts assumed the primary lead in the grant project. As chair of MSU's Department of Curriculum and Instruction, she carried considerable authority. Because she knew the people in the department, she was able to recruit individuals to become involved in MIE based on their experience and the project's needs. She followed up her recruiting with a talent that is difficult to develop: She resisted any urge to micromanage. Once she selected her coleaders, she left them alone to do their jobs and never second-guessed them. Amy's talent extended beyond delegating authority. She served as the connection between the project's leaders and the foundation, the grant's funding agency. If a delicate phone call was required, we all gladly deferred to Amy. She is a politician in the most positive sense: She is good with people.

Amy asked Karen Black to take the lead on the MSU side. Karen, an assistant professor in mathematics education, was in the final year of preparing to go up for tenure. She had several years of experience as a middle school mathematics teacher and a reputation as an excellent university instructor of elementary mathematics methods. She had also accomplished quite a bit within the MSU mathematics department, for example, successfully engineering new mathematics requirements for elementary education majors. But Karen had not been in a position, nor had the time, to concoct her dream mathematics elementary program. When she was asked to take charge of the university side of MIE, she felt unprepared. But her sense of duty coupled with her love of mathematics education propelled her into the project.

The university needed an active, enthusiastic leader to represent the schools. They found that in Grace Jordon, principal at Lincoln. With her regal manner and powerful voice, Grace commanded immediate attention. She was a dedicated advocate for the neighborhood in which she lived. She arrived at meetings early and left long after everyone else had gone home. She was tenacious and fought to get many resources for her school. She was aggressive in locating funding from the school district, universities, and local businesses. Like Amy, Grace had a lot on her plate. Grace ran a complex urban magnet school along with several large initiatives. She didn't have the time or background to write the grant for the MIE project. The task of representing the schools as the grant was developed was delegated to a Lincoln-Forest teacher.

I was that teacher. I had just started at Lincoln that fall. Although I had many years of elementary teaching experience in California, I had most recently worked in educational outreach for an agency at MSU. I was also a doctoral student in education at MSU. Lincoln and Forest were not unfamiliar to me. Both had hosted several of my "gee whiz" science programs. During those visits I had fantasized about teaching in one of the schools. As magnet schools, they had a dizzying array of resources. When the opportunity to teach at Lincoln arose, I jumped at it. Because of my connections with MSU, Grace made me the point person for this new grant. I was flattered both by Grace's confidence and Amy's enthusiastic reception of my involvement.

Putting Thoughts into Words

After the initial meeting, Karen and I became the leaders in the development of the proposal. Karen and I knew three things: We were writing the grant, the project focused on mathematics education, and the audience would be preservice and inservice teachers. The rest was up to us.

I asked Lincoln teachers what they wanted, in conversation and by sending out surveys. I got very little back. Teachers were overwhelmed and didn't want one more thing to think about. I asked to be put on the agenda for faculty meetings, but because there were so many ongoing projects the principal often forgot to include me or relegated me to the end, when teachers' energy was spent and everyone's primary motivation was to adjourn. I held after-school meetings with little success. Only two teachers regularly showed up, kindergarten teachers Pat and Wendy. Pat and Wendy came prepared to both protect themselves from any project mandates and to guarantee that kindergarten would be included thoughtfully in the plans. I was distressed that few people seemed to care about this opportunity. My distress was amplified by an early faculty meeting at Lincoln at which teachers were distinctly unenthusiastic. With a new literacy initiative, before- and after-school programs, magnet school obligations, and planning for a schoolwide discipline program, they had too much going on already. Until that meeting, I didn't know that Lincoln-Forest teachers taught an extra half-hour every day without compensation. That left them with more teaching to plan for and less time to plan it. Despite their reluctance, Lincoln teachers were at least aware of the project. I needed to make sure that the Forest teachers were informed as well.

My first meeting with Forest teachers was a trial. The meeting didn't start well—I was late. I had trouble finding the school, then finding my way around the maze of stairwells to the art room. When I arrived, the principal was nowhere to be seen. I didn't recognize anyone. A woman noticed my entrance and immediately introduced me, "You must be Chris Ohana. . . . She is here to speak to us about Lincoln's mathematics grant." Huh? Lincoln's grant? That was the first danger sign. The principal hadn't kept the staff informed. That might not have been his fault; I'm not sure that he was kept informed. I had planned my presentation on the assumption that the teachers at Forest were clued in about the project, but they knew absolutely nothing about MIE. I started by stating that we were submitting the grant application for Lincoln-Forest, not just Lincoln. There were some murmurs around the room, but the teachers listened.

As I presented Karen's and my ideas about the project, the teachers grew restless. Two in particular started asking questions. They took exception to the proposal to provide teachers with more planning time. Karen and I had configured the day with substitutes and creative scheduling available to relieve teachers so they could meet an extra hour or two per week to plan their mathematics program. Teachers never have enough time. I had assumed that providing more time would be a positive step. I couldn't have been more wrong. The Forest teachers resented the idea of spending any time out of the classroom and couldn't imagine how it would work. Who would take their classes? How could they make sure their classes were in good hands? How could they get everything done? There was a litany of objections. I tried to recover. I moved on, but the entire meeting had an antagonistic feel to it. The teachers wanted to know who would run the project. Where would the money go? It turned out that most of the Forest teachers thought I was from MSU, hence deserving of rough treatment. I also discovered that the teachers weren't getting messages about the MIE program. This meeting was as much a shock to them as it was to me.

I paid attention to all of the Forest teachers' concerns and came to certain conclusions: Teachers had to be given the choice to participate or not, and the project had to be integrated with their teaching lives. I saw it as part of my job to protect these teachers from "opportunities" they didn't want. I also concluded that the project's payoff had to be worth it. I wanted MIE to be a powerful agent in the school and not just window dressing. I believed that if we built the project with attention to teachers' time and talents, they would participate.

Meanwhile, Back at the University

Karen's task at the university was easier than mine in some respects, more difficult in others. The basic structure for the preservice teachers was already in place. LiC had been operating four years. Our year would be its fifth. Karen had to enlist just a couple of faculty members to give the cohort a "mathematics flavor." These faculty members would inject mathematics into their regular classes for MIE students, and they could also teach a few classes at Lincoln or Forest. But the few faculty members needed proved a challenge to recruit. Other MSU faculty members who taught in LiC were not mathematics focused. They had no investment in the MIE grant and no interest in teaching at Lincoln or Forest. And as an untenured assistant professor, Karen had no authority to require them to play along. So Karen became the only university member, aside from Amy, with a responsibility to the project. Amy essentially delegated the responsibility for writing the grant application to Karen. Ultimately, this ambitious project fell entirely on Karen's untenured shoulders and on me, a graduate student/teacher.

Putting Words onto Paper

So Karen and I set off to create a model teacher-preparation program in mathematics with all of the responsibility but little of the input or authority we needed. I immersed myself in the National Council of Teachers of Mathematics (NCTM) standards (1991). We both read article after article about preparing elementary school teachers to teach mathematics and we scoured the literature about mathematics instruction for information about university–school collaborations. In the end, we based our project proposal on the problems and solutions reported in the literature, assuming that our students and teachers were typical of those described.

When we asked for input from teachers, we had to ask in person. Few would respond to a survey. Unfortunately, the teachers' statements of their needs, essentially more supplies and manipulatives, didn't correspond to our observations or to research in the area. Research indicates that teachers need a deeper understanding of mathematics and how children come to learn mathematics. But we didn't want to dismiss what the teachers asked for. They had a legitimate need for more materials and for good, prepared lessons that would cut down on planning time. So Karen and I tried to weave the need for resources and the need for professional development together. We planned that MIE would provide calculators, lessons, and manipulatives to teachers who attended project workshops, hoping that by providing such support we would create an audience for project activities like study groups, classes, and action research. We set off to develop the project plan based on that hope.

We proposed that MIE would provide teachers with a continuum of opportunities. At the lowest level of involvement, Lincoln-Forest teachers would attend a few required inservices each year, many of which would be integrated with existing staff meetings. At a medium level of investment, teachers might work with a university student, attend a summer workshop or two, and participate in short-term study groups. At the deepest level of involvement, teachers might mentor university students, take workshops, work on an advanced degree or a mathematics endorsement, and participate in study and research groups. We worked out a veritable menu of options. We planned that teachers would be able to integrate mathematics throughout the curriculum by using grant-provided time and resources. Integrating mathematics with science, social studies, and reading would help all Lincoln-Forest teachers with their own curricula and would link their students' classroom experiences to mathematics. It would also encourage involvement from the broadest range of teachers, not just mathematics lovers. MIE would also pay for teachers to attend MSU courses and graduate programs, as well as to travel to regional and national NCTM meetings.

Karen and I proposed that the university's entire three-year preservice program be unified through a mathematics theme, reinforcing the idea that "Math Is Everywhere." Courses in educational foundations and multicultural education would all have a mathematics connection. The methods courses, which in LiC are usually taken in a four-course block of social studies, reading, mathematics, and science, would all include mathematics as a context.

The preservice students would also participate in extensive field experiences at Lincoln-Forest with elementary-level teachers who were engaged in deepening their own understanding of mathematics and mathematics teaching. Each preservice teacher would have a mentor at Lincoln or Forest who would help them negotiate the world of teaching.

"Math Is Everywhere" became our motto and name. Karen and I didn't choose it casually. We chose it because, from the beginning of the project, we thought it would encourage support from everyone, not just those who enjoyed teaching mathematics. If people can see mathematics everywhere, then reading teachers, physical education teachers, music teachers—*all* teachers—will realize that they also teach math. "Math Is Everywhere" summarizes Karen's and my favorite learning theory: Mathematics is learned best when its connections to real life are clear and abundant.

The project did get broad participation from many types of teachers at Lincoln and Forest. Resource teachers, a few reading teachers, science teachers, and most classroom teachers took some advantage of what MIE had to offer, which included a mathematics-based literature list and a study group on integrating math and reading. The talented art teacher received MIE funds to develop stronger connections between her art curriculum and mathematics.

Karen and I shared the ideal that MSU, Lincoln, and Forest staff members would become part of a blended team. We had both had experiences in elementary schools and at the university and we saw their potential for sharing with each other. We reasoned that if university faculty taught at Lincoln-Forest and elementary teachers taught parts of undergraduate courses, both would get insights into the needs and strengths of the other. We wrote the project grant to put money and resources into joint research projects. We believed that blending the university's research focus with actual classroom practice would make both stronger.

The Issues

In planning the project we could anticipate the tensions that often develop between university and elementary school staff cultures, and we recognized that issues of trust and control were inevitable. Other types of problems emerged as the project progressed.

Communication, Trust, and Leadership

Karen and I had high hopes of changing some aspects of institutional culture so that the worlds of the university and the schools could be blended. We knew that this deep and delicate transformation would require a dedication to developing communication, trust, and a new type of joint leadership.

Communication was critical. We needed support and input from elementary school teachers and administrators, MSU instructors and undergraduates, school district administrators, foundation representatives, and community members. Each group wanted to be kept informed, and they all wanted us to use different avenues of communication. Teachers, for example, admitted that they rarely read every piece of paper that was left in their mailboxes; they asked that we make brief oral presentations at faculty meetings. School district administrators preferred to receive brief memos with condensed summaries. They didn't want any surprises, but they didn't need details, either.

But communication involved more than the delivery of information. We also had to listen and respond to all the involved groups. This proved to be more difficult. We needed paths of communication that were open and public, but we also needed to keep certain information confidential. Balancing these two needs was tricky.

12

The preservice teachers wanted a voice as well. They knew that one goal of the project was to empower them as teachers. University faculty and elementary teachers would need to listen to these students and consider their ideas. It also became clear to Karen and me that we wouldn't get information from the Lincoln-Forest teachers unless they trusted us—and that trust wasn't automatic. The teachers needed to know that their feedback and suggestions were thoughtfully considered and a critical part of the information loop. They didn't want to invest time in thinking about the grant proposal and providing input if their ideas and energy were only being sought for reasons of public relations. We couldn't just ask for these teachers' input; we had to respond to them. By paying careful attention to listening and responding to all of these teachers' comments, we were slowly able to develop trust.

Teachers wanted the project leaders to trust and value what they know about their classrooms, their curricula and their children. The Lincoln-Forest teachers who were going to host student interns for long periods wanted to have a voice in the education of those preservice teachers. The MIE project leaders found that trust like this takes awhile to develop. The good news was, once teachers trusted us and the project, they were more forgiving of our mistakes.

The issues of communication and trust had immense consequences for the project leaders. Before we were able to establish open communication and trust, some members of the project's constituency said blunt and skeptical things about the project. Karen, Amy, and I had to listen carefully and develop thick skin so that the occasional barbs and criticisms would inform us, not deflate us. The initial stages, when we felt like we were buffeted from many directions, were especially tough. The university wants this, the teachers say that, the district says wait, the principals say go. We had to weave seemingly competing interests together and meet the needs of a variety of stakeholders while keeping our eyes on the overall project goals. It was a delicate process.

We also learned that a large-scale effort requires that someone "own" the project—that it be the priority for its leaders. But all leaders have many other responsibilities. A project needs a leader who can serve as an advocate, an apologist, and a contact person and for whom the project's goals and vision are the primary responsibility. No successful project can be managed from the periphery in someone's spare time: No one ever has spare time.

The Irony of Teacher Leadership in Reform

MIE was not a teacher-led initiative. Karen and I both started working on it as outsiders at Lincoln and Forest. I had organized and taught university outreach programs at the schools, then as soon as I became a Lincoln teacher, I plunged into this project with MSU. As a result, many teachers, especially at Forest, saw me as a university affiliate, not as one of their own. Karen had presented a few sessions at a summer workshop at Lincoln, but Lincoln and Forest teachers weren't the primary audience for that workshop. As an MSU professor she had taught mathematics methods to some of the newer Lincoln-Forest teachers; as a result, they regarded her as an authority figure rather than as a colleague.

A project like MIE needs leaders and coordinators who have a firm grasp of reform efforts, but such people are by definition outside of the mainstream of practice. It's ironic if we say we want to empower teachers but then recruit others, even other teachers, to tell them how they should change. Teachers must be trusted to know what they need, yet because many different measures of student achievement suggest that mathematics isn't being taught very well, it's clear that reform is needed. There's further irony in the fact that MSU recognized that preservice teachers and education faculty needed more experience in the classroom—yet the classrooms are in need of reform.

Where does the seed for change originate? Does the source matter? In our case that complicated question had a complicated answer, which is discussed in Chapter 3.

The Clash of Cultures and Values

Long before Karen and I started to develop the grant proposal, we were aware of differences in the cultures of the schools and the university. Despite our experiences in both settings, we found that the depth of these differences continually challenged our efforts.

The culture at Lincoln and Forest was shaped by a number of different issues. The teachers suffered from an ailment that's common to most U.S. teachers: an acute shortage of time and resources. They had little time to do much beyond teach and scramble to get ready for the next day. Planning time was scarce and had to be juggled with everything from administrative responsibilities to skinned knees and recess duty. Although Lincoln and Forest had a wealth of science materials, mathematics manipulatives had to be shared or created, so teachers had to compete for those resources.

The teachers were focused on their own classrooms, and they valued knowledge gained from classroom experience. They weren't overtly disparaging of research-generated knowledge, but they had little access to it or time to read it. The immediate needs of twenty-five children kept them plenty busy. Their primary, and at times overwhelming, responsibility was for the classroom learning environment. Their ultimate responsibility was for the growth of their own students. Any activities that didn't seem to support their immediate responsibilities had to pass a litmus test: It couldn't detract from their classroom lives and responsibilities.

The environment at MSU was different in fundamental ways. As at many universities, teaching took just a fraction of the professors' time. MSU faculty members had a deep investment in understanding, conducting, and publishing research, and they valued the knowledge generated by research. They listened to, and even respected, practitioner knowledge that was based on classroom experience, but they classified it as "anecdotal." Meetings, research analysis, reading, writing, teaching, and yet more meetings filled the professors' calendars. If spending time in an elementary classroom was going to be valuable enough to fit into their calendars, faculty members had to get something out of it that would be valued by their own promotion and tenure committees. That "something" would likely be research or grant funding. Spending the substantial time necessary to foster university–school collaborations would be professional suicide for these faculty members if the university structure didn't value it.

The preservice teachers added another element to the clash of cultures. Technically they represented the university, but they aspired to be part of the elementary schools' culture. They developed their own personality as a cohort. The undergraduates listened to the experience and advice of their mentor inservice teachers but trusted their own cohort more. And they depended on the university faculty for grades, placements, and letters of reference. They straddled both worlds but belonged in neither, so they created their own sets of values and beliefs.

Small Picture/Big Picture

Designing and administering the MIE project required that Karen and I attend to many details. We had to look at school district timelines and requirements, school calendars and schedules, university issues and budgets, grant deadlines, and the meeting dates of national professional organizations such as the NCTM. We were as careful as possible to anticipate and respond to the necessary details—we didn't want to be sloppy.

Our attention to detail had an unexpected result: We found ourselves becoming cynical and disappointed when small things didn't work as well as we had hoped. Focusing on the minutiae of the project led us to micromanage and microanalyze every shortcoming. A meeting didn't go as well as planned? We forgot to schedule a workshop to avoid conflicting with another event? Such small failings sometimes demoralized us, and we hit slumps.

Fortunately, Karen and I were occasionally able to sit back and look at the big picture. Writing annual reports to the foundation that administered the project grant helped us realize that we had, despite setbacks and disappointments, accomplished quite a bit. Our efforts to evaluate the MIE project also reenergized us. For example, when focus groups of teachers were interviewed by outside evaluators, most teachers said that they appreciated our efforts and many even reported that participation in the project was a "transformational" experience in their attitudes toward and confidence in teaching mathematics. Karen and I learned that, as important as the details are, it's critical to keep the bigger goals in sight.

As the project progressed, and we kept seeing accomplishments juxtaposed with shortcomings, Karen and I recognized that the project had its own life cycle, with predictable phases. The initial struggle to establish the project's identity and develop trust was followed by a giddy period in which things took off at lightning speed. As the project stabilized Karen and I did the less glamorous job of maintaining the program, which led to a stage of soul-searching and reevaluation in which we challenged our existing course and looked at alternatives that might recharge our energy.

Integrating Mathematics

Ironically, the project's goal of incorporating mathematics into all instruction sometimes diluted the mathematics focus. If math is everywhere and everyone is a math teacher, people wondered, why couldn't we use grant funds to send teachers to a technology conference? And if a technology conference was okay, why not an early childhood conference or a reading conference? If project funds could buy math manipulatives, how about some science supplies that could tie in to those manipulatives? Two teachers asked to buy a digital camera so they could document math work and motivate their students, but it wasn't clear how the camera would accomplish this.

In the long term, this loss of focus spread scarce project resources too thin. Those of us who came of age in the late '60s might remember the animated movie *The Point*. One line of dialogue applies here: "A point in every direction is the same as no point at all." In some areas of the MIE project, mathematics became a component of other subjects or topics rather than the organizing theme. The point was dulled.

Living on the Margins

Despite our hope that all the teachers at Lincoln and Forest and a contingent of university faculty members would become involved with the project, Karen and I had to become reconciled to the fact that MIE remained on the margins at Lincoln-Forest and MSU.

At MSU, this was a small program, set apart from the mainstream of teacher preparation. Most faculty members knew very little about it, and the few who did know either were ambivalent or expressed hostility because of the resources it commanded. MIE was definitely not center stage.

The undergraduate students who participated were isolated from their peers. They underwent their last three years of undergraduate education courses in a small cohort of twenty-one students. They traveled together, studied together, and taught together. Some even lived together. They had few chances to meet the broader range of students in the regular education program. Some other students saw this cohort as elitists and snobs.

Even at Lincoln and Forest, MIE's emphasis on mathematics education marginalized our efforts in some ways. Many first-grade teachers didn't feel that mathematics was a priority as they struggled to get their students to read. Some Reading Recovery and Title I and II reading teachers didn't see any advantage to MIE, and PE and music teachers were even less inclined to participate. Instead of permeating the schools, MIE was a side attraction.

Missing in Inaction

Despite project leaders' efforts to encourage wide participation in MIE, several perspectives were missing. We sought to bring in parents but had little success. Two parents came to some initial meetings. Communicating with them was difficult because they weren't part of the established loop within the schools and the university. We had made no coherent plan for parent participation. These parents rarely spoke at meetings, and in time they stopped coming. I cannot blame them.

The project also received little input from officials of the school district. Their involvement was sporadic and often focused on maintaining territory. They welcomed project resources—as long as they didn't interfere with normal operations. The district mathematics supervisor was at first understandably concerned that we not disturb the new and carefully crafted reform-based mathematics curriculum that she and her committee had worked long and hard to adopt. She was nervous about "improving" what had yet to be implemented. The district's evaluation office didn't want the university to use the schools as guinea pigs for some lame research project. This caution wasn't unreasonable: The mathematics supervisor and the evaluation office had had negative experiences with university partnerships in the past. They wanted to protect the schools, teachers, and children from any possible exploitation, and understandably so. But the district officials' lack of participation in MIE made it daunting for us to construct a reform effort that needed to simultaneously maintain the status quo.

The following chapters present the details of the MIE project to further highlight the major issues we encountered as we tried to improve the mathematics education of elementary students and inservice and preservice teachers. Since one major goal was to integrate the two elementary schools with the university, it's ironic that I found that the most productive way to organize the book was by having a chapter on each major group: inservice teachers, preservice teachers, and the university. In the end, we all had separate roles in the project. Our success came from respecting boundaries, not from crossing them.

2

Teacher Learning and
Teacher Leadership

With Janet Sharp

As I write this, I am struck by the ambition of our MIE project. We were trying to integrate better mathematics learning in elementary school classrooms with teacher leadership in the education of preservice teachers. To make progress in either area would have been formidable, but we intended do both. We wanted to simultaneously improve teachers' learning of mathematics and develop and use teacher expertise in the professional preparation of new teachers. Working classroom teachers would become an integral part of preservice education. Preservice students would be placed in classrooms where quality mathematics learning occurred and where the teachers would model mathematics instruction that led to children's understanding and appreciation of mathematical ideas. University faculty would be in touch with classroom teachers' daily lives, translate and interpret research for practitioners, and understand and address the needs of elementary school teachers and their students. The result would be a whole system that was able to meet the needs of inservice teachers, preservice teachers, and elementary school students.

The scenario we imagined was based on several assumptions:

- Classroom teachers would want to be part of preservice teacher education. The project would give them the time that was necessary to integrate preservice teachers into their routine.
- Classroom teachers would want to learn more about mathematics education and to share their knowledge with each other and with preservice teachers. They would stretch and develop their own understanding of mathematics.

- Classroom teachers and university faculty members would trust each other enough to develop an intimate working relationship. Because we were asking teachers to share the responsibility for preservice education, teachers who participated had to trust that the university faculty they worked with would take their needs and suggestions seriously.

This chapter explores these and related issues.

Time

Lincoln and Forest teachers arrive at school before 8:00, if they can, for a school day that begins at 9:15. They stream in with armfuls of stuff looking like well-dressed bag ladies. They check their mailboxes, then head toward their rooms, having several short hallway conversations on the way. Once a teacher is in her room, she glances at the day's schedule and then starts pulling out reading books for the morning and organizing them for groups. She flips through her plans again: Oh, shoot—the class needs paper and Geoboards for math, too. She rushes to find them, but before she's halfway done it's time to pick the kids up at the door. Except for a ten-minute recess, during which she'll get the rest of the math materials, this teacher will get no break until lunch. And this is a calm day. On other days there might be a "short" meeting before school, or breakfast duty or bus duty.

This typical schedule points out a primary obstacle to intensive study and reflective practice: U.S. teachers suffer from a profound deficit of time. The school day is long and planning time is very short. Lincoln and Forest were also site-based management schools, which increased the demands on teachers' time. Meetings, classes—we did it all. Could grant money create more time for professional development? Karen and I knew that there was little after-school or before-school time for development, so the only time to do things was during the school day. In the initial proposal we budgeted resources to hire substitutes so that teachers would be able to get together in grade-level groups to discuss curriculum, review assessments, or study. We also proposed that a graduate student with a teaching license be hired to help out through substituting or assuming other duties, like recess supervision, that would release teachers to spend more time on teaching or learning mathematics.

21

Once the project began, carving out time for teachers to meet proved to be more difficult than Karen and I had thought. It was a herculean task to orchestrate the substitutes. Whose classes would they cover? When? Where? Teachers wanted us to avoid scheduling project meetings during their music, art, and PE times as well. Many teachers, especially those at Forest, didn't want to be released from their classes. The effort involved wasn't worth it to them. They objected that writing substitute plans is a time-consuming task, plus, substitutes rarely do as good a job as the regular teacher does. Learning would suffer—and learning was their highest priority. Even when staff development meetings did take place, teachers just did what they were accustomed to doing: planning. Not the type of deep planning that's needed to teach more effectively, but the type of planning that's necessary, but purely logistical: Who is getting the pumpkins for Halloween? Is someone running off the permission slips for the field trip?

With a finite amount of time in the school day, a teacher can take on only so many things. There are many "opportunities" for teachers—activities that can sap both time and energy. Some are necessary and productive. Some are not. A teacher has to pick and choose to the degree that she can. With an aggressive principal who attracted money like a magnet, Lincoln already had a smorgasbord of programs and activities that demanded teachers' attention when Karen and I began planning MIE, and several new major initiatives were starting. One was an early literacy program that was highly structured and required a considerable investment of time. All the teachers in the program were required to take a demanding reading instruction course that met once a week, immediately after school, for three hours and that involved a series of assignments in a text and practice in their classrooms. Teachers complained about the time commitment, but they had no choice. In writing this, five years after the beginning of MIE, I am amazed that our project leaders entertained the idea of starting a big new professional development project as another one was just beginning. What were we thinking? But that wasn't all: We also began a new behavior management program at the same time. In addition, teachers were under pressure to make the school more of a magnet—that is, to actually teach science. The teachers were, to say the least, stressed. By creating MIE, we were putting yet more pressure on them.

Karen and I tried to relieve that pressure by offering many options. Table 1 shows the variety of professional development activities MIE offered, their purpose, the time commitment required, and any compensation teachers received for participating. The activities are listed roughly in order of the amount of time they required of teachers.

TABLE 1. *Professional Development Activities for Classroom Teachers*

Activity	Purpose	Participation	Time Commitment and Compensation
Faculty meetings	To learn or review basic information about mathematics standards.	Required for all MIE teachers.	Minimal, and during regular school hours.
Workshops	To learn more about or practice using specific classroom-focused materials and information (basic facts, calculator use, use of manipulatives, etc.).	Voluntary. Each workshop had 6–20 participants.	2–4 two-hour meetings after school. Teachers were paid or received classroom materials.
Summer workshops and institutes	To learn more about pedagogy and get teaching ideas, such as by using Marilyn Burns workshops.	Voluntary. 5–15 teachers were involved each summer.	24–80 hours per workshop. Tuition paid.
Hosting preservice teachers in field work	To model and teach instruction techniques.	Voluntary. 20 Lincoln-Forest teachers per semester.	Variable—about 2 hours per week for practicum, 6 hours per week for student teacher. Small stipend for host teacher.
National or regional math educator meetings	To learn more about math education standards, teaching practices, and other professional issues.	Voluntary. 3–10 teachers per meeting.	3–5 days. Registration, transportation, and per diem paid.

(continues)

TABLE 1. *(continued)*

Activity	Purpose	Participation	Time Commitment and Compensation
Mini-conferences	To exchange teaching ideas through presentations.	All MIE teachers required to attend. About 8 did presentations at each miniconference.	Presenters: 6 hours of preparation and presentation time per presentation. Attendees: 1 hour per miniconference.
Study groups	To research and learn about math teaching and learning.	Voluntary. 4–12 teachers per group.	6 hours of meeting time plus 12 hours of research and reading time. Paid hourly.
University courses	To learn mathematics and pedagogy.	Voluntary. 6–12 teachers per semester.	Extensive time needed to attend and do assignments for graduate course. Tuition and books paid.
University teaching	To teach undergraduate math education students and to do research in support of math education.	Voluntary. 1–3 teachers per semester. 4 teachers were involved through life of grant.	Extremely intensive time commitment. Paid as an adjunct professor for each course taught.

Faculty Meetings, Workshops, and Professional Meetings

At the most minimal level of commitment, MIE teachers wouldn't have to do any more than come to faculty meetings during school hours. We carved out some time during these meetings to give teachers information about Karen's inservices and to offer general introductions to the National Council of Teachers of Mathematics (NCTM) standards. Other short-term commitments included two-hour after-school workshops on specific topics such as calculator use and strategies for teaching basic number facts. Teachers who were willing to commit more of their time were encouraged to attend a local, regional, or national mathematics conference or to attend a summer workshop by Marilyn Burns or Kathy Richardson.

Hosting Preservice Teachers in Field Work

Karen and I hoped that playing a key role in the professional development of preservice teachers would also contribute to the professional development of the Lincoln-Forest teachers: that the teachers would learn things that the undergraduate students were learning and that the students would learn from the teachers' experience. But the learning turned out to be one-sided. The students picked up a lot from being in the classroom, and they expressed their appreciation for the experience over and over. But the classroom teachers didn't, with a few exceptions, say that they learned much from the students. A couple of Forest teachers said that they enjoyed having the preservice teachers in their classroom because it kept them on their toes. They were sure to plan carefully when they were modeling for the preservice teachers. But few mentioned learning from the preservice teachers.

Miniconferences

Professional knowledge gained from workshops and other professional development events often remains private knowledge because teachers lack the time, incentive, or opportunity to share what they've learned. The MIE project provided a partial solution to this by using miniconferences in which Lincoln and Forest teachers and university faculty members could present something that they had learned from a workshop or conference that they had been sponsored to attend. Miniconferences replaced regular faculty meetings twice a year. Each miniconference was divided into three thirty-minute periods, with a variety of presentations taking place simultaneously during each. Some of the presentations were for primary-grade teachers and others were for teachers of upper grades. Presentations covered many mathematics strands and topics. Teachers, principals, and university professors were all pleased with this activity. Teachers liked it because they got something practical out of it. It was convenient, it was short, and there was choice about what to learn. University faculty liked the chance to be students instead of presenters. They sat in sessions with classroom teachers and we were all learners together, blurring for a moment the barriers between the university and the schools.

The beauty of putting on a miniconference is that it is simple and free. Any school could do it. Our organizational time was minimal and the teachers' time investment was small. To prepare a miniconference, I simply looked at the list of teachers who had attended workshops and other mathematics-related professional development opportunities and asked them to share one lesson that they had learned at that workshop and had success with in the classroom. Teachers used activities they already knew and used so the miniconference took little extra planning from them. Some teachers were nervous about presenting to their peers, but virtually everyone experienced a high afterward that came from success, appreciation from their colleagues, and a sense of professionalism. Many of us wondered if such miniconferences couldn't be a regular replacement for standard faculty meetings.

Study Groups

In the second year of the MIE project, I floated the idea of study groups. Study groups are based on several assumptions:

- Teachers deserve more control of their own professional development. They know best what it is they need to become better teachers.
- Teachers will benefit from working with each other. Collectively they will have the knowledge and skills to help each other.
- Having a chance to reflect on current practice will lead teachers to change their practice.

The idea to implement study groups came from a number of sources. I was particularly interested in the work that Carne Barnett at WestEd did on study groups on fractions (Barnett, Goldenstein, and Jackson 1994). After hearing a research presentation about the work, I was sure it was a great idea. I wanted to teach in a school where teachers routinely read about, tried, and shared ideas. Study groups have huge possibilities for learning and teaching. I thought the MIE project could have study groups about assessment or about curriculum integration of mathematics. The ideas were limitless.

It is embarrassing to admit now that I thought study groups were a great idea. The idea got little buy-in from the teachers, and the study groups weren't very successful.

When teachers were presented with the idea that the project could support them in forming groups to study issues they wanted to learn more about, they were uncertain of what such groups would look like or what they could offer. After some prodding and suggestions, teachers said they wanted to learn more about calculators, manipulatives, and integrating literature into math classes. Then they made suggestions about who could lead them. The district supervisor was a calculator expert. She could teach us about the proper use of calculators. Karen knew lots about manipulatives. She could lead that group. Most of the study groups turned into workshops because that was the structure the teachers understood.

One exception was a group that formed around integrating children's literature with mathematics. It was spearheaded by a Lincoln teacher who organized the group and scheduled its meetings. The group members developed a product: a list of children's books at Lincoln's library that related to math topics in the curriculum. Rather than really studying anything, this group evolved into a work group.

I am still optimistic about the possibilities for and benefits of study groups, but I learned that my approach was off base. If the goal is to develop greater teacher leadership, ideas have to come from the teachers. The benefits of an activity have to be visible and valuable. In retrospect, I believe that Karen and I should have constructed a study group, had teachers lead it, and then had them conduct a cost/benefit analysis of the activity. Was it worth it? The teachers have to decide. What is worth studying? Again, teachers have to develop the ideas. If they don't, the goal of teacher leadership is compromised.

University Courses

At a higher level of commitment to the MIE project, some teachers chose to take university classes from Karen. The classes could count toward a master's degree or a mathematics teaching endorsement. It was no easy feat for Karen to prepare and teach classes that served both purposes. The classes carried graduate credits in the mathematics department, but the mathematics was more basic than what is expected of a graduate course in mathematics. Teachers started with a semester-long course in the teaching of algebra. Content was blended with pedagogy, but the content itself was at the level of basic algebra that one might teach in elementary school. The focus was on having the teachers understand that content at a deep level. Karen's assumption in designing these courses was similar to the one that Liping Ma (1999) describes as guiding the education of elementary teachers in China: Specialized high-level mathematics courses may not help elementary teachers teach better. Instead, they need to understand the mathematics they teach and the connections between mathematics areas. And they must understand how to develop those concepts in their students. Karen's first challenge was to convince her colleagues in MSU's mathematics department of this assumption because they had to agree to offer her classes through the department. The second obstacle was to get enough students. There were a few teachers who would take almost any course that Karen might offer. Some were motivated by the desire to get an elementary math endorsement. Others simply enjoyed mathematics. All of them wanted to learn how to teach mathematics better. But these few students were not enough to justify offering a college course. I used a variety of techniques to convince Lincoln-Forest teachers to take the classes—including begging. Some were easy to persuade: They needed some graduate credit and they liked Karen. A few were a harder sell. I called in a few favors. I made some promises. We ended up with enough students to offer the course. We repeated this pattern in the following semesters.

University Teaching

The most demanding and time-consuming of the MIE professional development activities was to teach at the university. Several teachers, myself included, were invited to teach entire courses. I taught science methods to the LiC cohort. Jane, a reading specialist, was asked to teach language arts and reading. And Kirk, a first/second-grade teacher, was hired to teach mathematics methods for early childhood educators. We were all armed with some potent pedagogical ammunition—real classroom stories—but we also committed large chunks of time to learning more about the research in our fields. We felt responsible for teaching current research-supported information to our university classes. It was unnerving to stare at a roomful of young adults who were writing down what we said. We worked at deserving their trust.

This was probably the most effective of all the MIE professional development activities in terms of blending practice and research, but it was also the most inefficient. It affected only three elementary school teachers and it changed nothing about the university. To make matters worse, all three of us left the school system. Jane is still teaching as an adjunct at the university. Kirk left Lincoln to work with the state department of education. And I am firmly embedded in higher education research and teaching. This activity will have no trickle-down effect on the other teachers. It might have been better if the three of us had each cotaught with a university professor. That would have reduced the pressure of the commitment and may have encouraged more teachers to try it. As it developed, the commitment was so intense that only those who were trying university teaching on as a possible career change were tempted to do it. If teachers had been able to coteach with professors, it may have been less threatening. It would also have led to some professional development for university faculty members and some cross-fertilization of experiences from the elementary school and research worlds. But as this activity evolved, the growth it led to remained the private experience of the three of us who went on to leave the school system.

In the end, the project wasn't successful in creating more professional development time for teachers. For the Lincoln-Forest teachers, more time out of the classroom was neither possible nor desirable. The project was, however, able to accomplish the next-best thing: We respected teachers' time by offering them a range of possibilities for participating in MIE. Teachers could, for the most part, choose to participate or not. Even within required activities, such as the miniconferences, we still provided choice and tried to accommodate the interests of everyone. The teachers appreciated this; they weren't accustomed to being able to exercise that much choice.

The amount of choice we provided did have a negative side. Because all the participants bought into the project at different levels, we were unable to create a learning community in the ways we had hoped. Some teachers got a lot out of the four years but many others did not. Knowledge remained as it had been—in the private reserve of individual teachers.

Trust

We know that effective professional development for mathematics instructors teaches mathematics, models sound teaching techniques, and requires teachers to analyze teaching and learning. The MIE project offered a range of activities to nurture teacher development, but getting Lincoln-Forest teachers to participate required the project leaders to develop teachers' trust of MSU's efforts.

The teachers at Lincoln and Forest represented a range of interests and skills. As in any other group of people, some were eager to learn new things while others were more cautious. The MIE enthusiasts included classroom teachers as well as mathematics specialists. They committed themselves to participating in just about every project activity, taking every university course, attending every workshop, and traveling to many conferences. In the end, at least two earned elementary mathematics endorsements from the state. There were also regular classroom teachers who availed themselves of most of the project opportunities. For the most part, these were upper-grade teachers at Forest. Two others, a technology teacher at Forest and Forest's assistant principal (who was also a teacher), assumed many project leadership functions, attending planning meetings and helping to teach workshops, as well as taking classes themselves.

For some of the Lincoln-Forest teachers, the most valuable aspects of MIE were increased access to manipulatives, travel to conferences, and access to instructional technology. Even though our schools had an enviable level of resources for the science magnet program, classroom teachers still had to share equipment or materials, make their own, or go without. Many teachers were eager to attend professional meetings such as NCTM conferences and Marilyn Burns workshops. Those who saw the project this way were more tentative in their response to MIE. They wanted to know explicitly what would be expected of them in return.

What strings were attached? Who would keep track of the money? How much material could each teacher get? Who would decide who got to go to professional meetings? What commitment was expected?

I found this distrustful attitude maddening. I bristled at the suggestion that there might be strings attached, or that a clique of favorite Lincoln teachers would reap all the rewards. But when I forced myself to stop being defensive, it was easy to see why so many teachers were tentative about MIE. They had had many experiences of their views and their work being first solicited and then neglected. For instance, control over the magnet school resources was a closely guarded secret. No one except the principals knew where the money went. Teachers got extra field trips and a modest grade-level budget, but had no control of or knowledge about how positions were allocated or how the rest of the money, about $50,000 per school each year, was spent. This secrecy bred suspicions and rumors. Like Elvis, magnet school and MIE project monies were spotted everywhere: paying for lunches, books, artwork, and travel. Providing certain teachers with extra income. It would be an exaggeration to say that I was scared to show up with new clothes for fear they might fan the flames of suspicion, but the thought did cross my mind.

It would have been easy to dismiss these fears and suspicions as petty and provincial if they weren't so prevalent and an issue at both Lincoln and Forest. Resistance to the MIE project came from among the best and most dedicated teachers at the two schools, the ones who worked long hours, were willing to share, and wanted to learn. The project leaders couldn't and didn't want to work around them: These teachers had to be the core of those who were involved.

Some teachers weren't necessarily distrustful or suspicious, they were just uninterested. Some of these were language arts specialists in Title I reading or Reading Recovery programs, but a few were regular classroom teachers. They were busy with their teaching and their lives and did not have the energy or interest to get involved. They didn't want, or feel the need, to spend time after school in study groups or classes. They already had enough meetings: Between faculty meetings, district meetings, grade-level meetings, and committee meetings, they were booked. When were they supposed to get ready for tomorrow? They didn't feel any special urge to devote more time to mathematics teaching, much less to taking an algebra class. Some made it quite clear that they did not teach math, or that reading was their priority. Their message was definite: Don't waste my time.

I was less bothered by the disinterested teachers than by the suspicious ones. The disinterested ones were relatively few in number and somewhat marginal to the project because of their almost exclusive involvement with reading. I would have preferred to count them among those involved with MIE, but I understood that they had other commitments and interests. My hope was that we could develop some programs that would pique their interest. I was more concerned about the teachers who feared that their time and energy would be drained to no advantage. There is perhaps no greater offense to a teacher than to waste her time. We needed to reduce this suspicion and create an environment in which teachers would create their own journey toward improving their practice. The road to greater trust was long and complicated, and required that the project leaders use a number of strategies.

Communicating

It seems obvious that communication would be critical to building trust. But knowing that and addressing it are different. What is the best way to communicate with teachers? And how can they communicate with you?

Karen and I made early plans for communicating with the Lincoln-Forest teachers. We went with two basic models: a newsletter and discussion at faculty meetings. The newsletter was distributed monthly. I wrote most of it. It detailed upcoming classes and events. Although it was only two pages long, it turned out to not be a wise investment of time and paper. There's a simple explanation for that: Look at a teacher's mailbox. Each day a teacher does major triage while going through mail. If a piece of mail isn't critical, it gets tossed. Our MIE newsletter usually met the latter fate. Only the true believers read it.

Communicating at faculty meetings wasn't much better. Our time to announce MIE matters usually came at the end of a packed agenda. Teachers were anxious to get out and there was a certain amount of peer pressure to not ask questions. And many teachers missed part or all of a faculty meeting.

I switched tactics in the second year of the project, trying to attend grade-level meetings. This didn't prove to be much more effective. The meetings usually targeted upcoming plans—field trips, curriculum planning, and so on. There wasn't any time to devote to MIE. And because I had to repeat the same spiel for each grade, this method was inefficient.

So if we couldn't communicate during faculty meetings, through a newsletter, or at grade-level meetings, what could we do? One method that was effective was to place announcements on the school message board. Everyone looked at it daily to see who was absent and what the day's meetings were. But the message board could only be used for short announcements such as opportunities for conferences and undergraduate visits, so we could communicate only so much this way.

Electronic mail might have been helpful, but we didn't use it. At mid-project we were just at the point where all of the teachers had email accounts, but most were not yet comfortable using email. I'm now involved in a project for which we communicate regularly through email. Just like any other method, it works with some teachers but not others.

Karen and I found that one-on-one visits were one of our most effective methods of communication. We communicated as we traveled the halls, ran into people, and wandered into classrooms. Informal conversations were good for sharing things, asking favors, and offering services. They weren't good for communicating policy issues, but most of our communication was more mundane.

The key was to have multiple lines of communication. We found that no single method was enough by itself, but by using many methods we were able to keep everyone informed. At times our communication was redundant, but some redundancy was important. It ensured that everyone who needed information got it.

Communication about the project wasn't a one-way street. Karen and I depended on teachers to tell us if they liked something or not. We hoped to get their input and give them a voice in making decisions. But despite our honest intent to have a dialogue, we didn't think to provide a formal structure for teacher input. That was a mistake. Some teachers felt comfortable sharing their opinions with us privately, but others didn't. As a consequence, I heard things secondhand or through the rumor mill.

Admitting Errors—and Not Repeating Them

It's easy to become defensive when you make an error in public. But it's better to go on the offensive in a positive way. Admit the error and move on. Otherwise, the error takes on a life of its on. To make sure people know it was an honest mistake, try not to commit the same error again. One of the errors Karen and I made was in determining which teachers would teach at the university. We didn't open up the process; we handpicked a teacher. Some other teachers were livid. Why weren't they considered? When I heard the rumblings, my first reaction was to defend our choice: We had to have someone with a master's degree and who was comfortable with math. But then I realized, painfully, that the teachers were right. What if I were in their shoes? I would be equally upset at the thought of a private process that excluded people. We had had a lapse of judgment and been inconsiderate. We admitted our error, and in order to avoid making the same mistake, developed a procedure for applying for university teaching positions.

Extending Before Requesting

We were constantly asking teachers to do something: take a class, host a student teacher, attend a conference. But we also extended the project to them. Karen was eager to demonstrate lessons in teachers' classrooms. We offered access to materials. I taught people's classes so they could get ready to present at a miniconference. These efforts provided teachers with proof that we were trying hard and working as hard as they were. We weren't asking more of them than we would give.

Being Visible

Karen and I knew that if the MIE project was to become a true university–school partnership, we would need to be visible. I was certainly present at both the university and Lincoln, but I taught at Lincoln, so it was hardly remarkable that I was seen there. Karen tried to be visible to school faculty. She guest taught in classrooms. She gave workshops. But she could do only so much because she was up for tenure, and there's no tenure evaluation category for "being visible in schools." What about other MSU faculty? The university was forty miles away from the schools and the distance created a barrier. No other faculty members had the investment in MIE that Karen had. As a result, only about three of the eight or nine LiC cohort faculty ever set foot in Lincoln or Forest, and only one participated in coteaching or attended meetings at the schools. This eroded the elementary teachers' trust because it looked like the university didn't find the project as important as the schools did. Much of the work that was being accomplished by the university faculty wasn't visible to the school staffs. Since it wasn't seen, it couldn't be valued. This led teachers to the logical conclusion that the university got more from the project than it gave. It didn't help elevate our level of trust.

Listening and Respecting

My family once asked me to get a hearing test. I did. It turned out that I wasn't hard-of-hearing: I was hard-of-listening. If our project was to avoid this problem, Karen and I had to develop listening skills and not just communicate, but hear, listen, and respond respectfully. We tried to deal with problems as they arose. Since we had no official line of communication from teachers, we had to use less-direct ways to listen. Once we heard something, directly or indirectly, we responded. We tried to develop workshops around teachers' interests, we answered questions, and we sought information. We did everything we could to accommodate teachers' expressed interests.

Occasionally this led to conflicts. What if one teacher wants to do something that's in conflict with the goals of the project? We sometimes approved purchases or project activities, such as study groups, that had little to do with math teaching or learning. We were ambivalent about them, but we approved them for several reasons. First, teachers justified them in terms of their math teaching. We wanted to respect their decisions. Second, we wanted teachers to use the project and consider the things they might need to teach better. Third, if we wanted teachers to feel like part of the decision making, we had to give them the authority to make decisions. Karen and I needed to trust their decisions as we asked them to trust ours, even if we disagreed with what they wanted.

Providing Choice

The choice that the project afforded teachers led to a growing level of trust. We told teachers that they could participate in any project activities they wanted to—or in none at all. This flexibility proved to be critical. Teachers valued the opportunity to construct their own involvement, and they did get involved—usually we got as many teachers to participate in an activity as we needed. Occasionally I would have to do a sales job to get enough teachers to host MSU students, but I rarely worried about teacher involvement. Offering choices is really an extension of teacher decision making: If we trust teachers, we have to trust it when they say no.

The trust that developed among Karen, the Lincoln-Forest teachers, and I was critical to the MIE project. It allowed Karen and me to ask for input and participation without making the teachers feel coerced. It created a positive environment for the project and made Karen's and my jobs easier in the long run.

Teachers' Beliefs and Values

Many education reform efforts of the past decade have advocated for transferring decision-making authority to teachers (Weiss 1995). The MIE project anticipated such a shift of authority. One project goal was for the university to share the responsibility of preservice teacher education with inservice teachers. Inservice teachers have a great wealth of knowledge that is often lost in university-based preservice courses, and we wanted to tap in to that resource so the Lincoln-Forest teachers could share their understanding of teaching with the preservice students. Those who possess practical professional knowledge deserve a voice in the preparation of teachers. A second major project goal was to have classroom teachers grow in their understanding of mathematics and in ways to teach mathematics for greater student understanding and enjoyment. We assumed that teachers valued and would want to help shape preservice education, and that they wanted to learn more mathematics.

But were our goals consistent with what the teachers actually valued? While it's dangerous to overgeneralize, most of the Lincoln-Forest teachers shared a core set of beliefs. These beliefs, shaped by both personality and work environment, affected their reception of MIE.

Student Learning

One of the most visible of the teachers' core values was their passion for student learning. It's deceptively simple: Teachers teach and students learn, and student learning and students' attitudes toward learning are teachers' primary concern. But at Lincoln-Forest, all learning was not created equal. Teachers wanted their students to learn and enjoy mathematics, but the top priority wasn't mathematics, it was reading. Most of the teachers at Forest and Lincoln, whatever their core teaching role, were comfortable being reading teachers, but they didn't identify themselves as mathematics teachers.

Preservice Teacher Education

What about our hope that classroom teachers would share responsibility for preparing preservice teachers? While the teachers valued preservice teacher education, they had little interest in and weren't motivated to take an active role in developing the preservice teacher component of the project. Teachers saw their duty and professional responsibility as being to teach their own classrooms. They each had twenty-five children to teach. They didn't feel it was part of their job to also teach university students: "Isn't that what we pay the university professors to do?" Several of the university faculty members who were scheduled to teach the LiC cohort surveyed the teachers about what they thought should be included in the preservice course. The teachers were virtually silent—with one exception, they had no suggestions for those who were teaching the preservice classes. The exception was with the university's reading methods instructor, whose mailbox overflowed with responses. There were two reasons for that: The first was that the instructor had been a popular reading coordinator at Lincoln. The second was that the teachers were more comfortable with reading instruction than with math or science instruction.

Resources

The classroom teachers valued the access to materials like manipulatives and calculators that the project gave them. Teachers are known for their desire to have more activities and lessons: "Give

me something I can do on Monday." People who provide professional development activities, especially university-based instructors, sometimes disparage this. We know that more lessons and
manipulatives won't by themselves improve student learning, but
it's arrogant to think that this value of teachers is unfounded.
Where does this value come from? It may be a by-product of other
values: Teachers value learning in their classrooms, so they want
materials they can use in their classrooms. Teachers need resources to meet their highest goal: student learning. Lessons and
activities are a resource. Teachers are desperate for time. Project
teachers' wish lists included things like classroom sets of math
rods and pattern blocks because they didn't want to spend their
most precious resource, time, making manipulatives. Packaged
lessons save time. Teachers' thirst for "stuff" is reasonable given
their lack of time and resources, and if teachers value student
learning and are short of time, their appreciation for pre-prepared
lessons is understandable.

Teachers also valued human resources. Project teachers saw the
university faculty and preservice teachers as a reservoir of help for
their own struggling students: More adults meant more attention
for students. Preservice teachers contributed to elementary students' learning by tutoring or teaching small groups.

Respect

Once upon a time, teachers enjoyed respect from the community.
Along with ministers and police, teachers were models of public
service and knowledge. Although the decline of respect for teachers is much more pronounced in the policy realm than in public
opinion, where parents still rank their own neighborhood schools
highly, teachers suffer from the decline in respect. Perhaps for this
reason, they are now more assertive in their expectations than
teachers used to be. Teachers value respect and they see financial
remuneration as one indication of respect. If more time and effort
are required, they expect to be reimbursed. The MIE project leaders wanted to show teachers that we respected their time and efforts, so we built in financial rewards for participation. Virtually
every professional development activity carried some extra pay. For
any inservice that occurred after contract hours, teachers received
overtime pay. This was a huge burden on the project budget. It also
created some tensions. Some teachers would sign up simply for the

money. We project leaders were troubled at the idea of offering such an extrinsic reward for becoming, we hoped, better teachers. In the long run, I'm glad we offered teachers compensation. It told them that we valued their time. If the practice was abused by some, so what? It did a greater good. On a grand scale, perhaps it would be better to pay teachers more and expect them to participate in continuing professional development, even if it meant postcontract hours. But the project was in no position to change teacher contracts and offer higher salaries. We did the best we could given the system, and teachers appreciated the compensation. Twenty dollars an hour was a small sum to pay to demonstrate respect.

Experience

Teachers live the phrase "Experience is the best teacher." They learn from their own experiences in the classroom and from listening to the stories of others. They value this firsthand experience more than any other professional activity. At Lincoln and Forest, while real classroom-based experience was valued, research was not—it was seen as removed from real experience. Karen and I realized that classroom teachers wouldn't transform into academic researchers. We never intended such a thing. We hoped, though, to encourage an interest in classroom-based research. The best teachers already analyzed their own teaching. What would happen if we blended their reflective teaching with research on teaching and learning? We knew such an effort would require some trust, so we waited. When we had a critical mass of teachers who would try something simply because Karen and I asked, we tried a study group. The group included fourth- and fifth-grade teachers from Forest and focused on fractions, ratios, and percents. Each teacher was paired with a university faculty member. The intent was to develop a joint-action research project. The university faculty member could help with research design and finding relevant literature. The classroom teacher could develop the questions and serve as the expert on applying the findings in the classroom. The design was full of promise. It made sense and linked the worlds of higher education and elementary education in a way that could advance both. But it wasn't successful. The university folks didn't know the classroom teachers, and they had their own agenda, which differed from both Karen's and the classroom teachers'. The classroom teachers were difficult to motivate

39

and many didn't develop a clear personal investment in the idea. The idea was good, but the combination of personalities was difficult because participants' goals didn't match. It may have been better if we had allowed research questions to grow from the classroom and then matched an appropriate professor with the classroom teacher based on the professor's interests and expertise and on personality. At least one of the professors was interested in postmodern philosophy, a body of literature that is difficult to digest and translate into ratios and percents. Karen and I liked the idea of study groups involving teachers and professors, but the pairings should have been more natural and comfortable. And perhaps the faculty-teacher pairings should have been dropped in favor of a teacher focused study group on teaching fractions.

Egalitarianism

The Lincoln and Forest teachers wanted the project to give them the same advantages it gave the university faculty, and they wanted all of the opportunities to be available to every teacher. This egalitarian ethic manifests in a number of contexts. Merit pay is one. Merit pay is a difficult concept for some teachers because it violates their belief that all teachers should be treated the same—no one is "better" than another. Karen and I tried, for the most part successfully, to make every MIE opportunity an open invitation. If there were activities, like attending the NCTM conference, that could accommodate only a small group, we needed clear selection criteria. This was difficult but probably helpful. Most teachers felt comfortable with knowing that they could participate or not—at their discretion, not ours.

The dedication to egalitarianism, however necessary, also had drawbacks. There were times when project funds were limited and Karen and I wanted to choose the participants who would either give the most to the project or gain the most professionally. But sometimes we were forced to choose people simply because we hadn't picked them for something else. We had to spread the wealth. This was true of some student practicum assignments: The university students were sometimes placed with teachers for political reasons. Margaret was a fifth-grade teacher who was difficult to work with and didn't have a positive reputation with other teachers. But she always asked for a practicum student or a student teacher. It became impossible to ignore her requests, so she received a practicum student. In trying to be fair to Margaret, we weren't fair to the student, who had a miserable semester. There were other times that our attempts to be egalitarian had negative consequences. Some teachers were chosen for tasks against our better judgment, and they lived up to our expectations. There were teachers sent to meetings who were required to come back and share but never did. There were teachers paid to develop a lesson or other product but never produced. But just as one of these experiences started to make me cynical, there would be a pleasant surprise. One teacher, Regina, wasn't known for going out of her way to help or participate. But one event, a math conference for early childhood, caught her attention. She asked to go and subsequently became a project convert.

Overlapping Goals

Despite the fact that we could have done better, our plans succeeded in generating trust and even enthusiasm from the elementary school teachers. Teachers, in interviews and casual comments, indicated that they appreciated the level of choice given to them. I wish that Karen and I had been less defensive, however. We started out by assuring teachers that we wouldn't waste their time. But not wasting time is not a powerful motivator. We should have started with what teachers value. What motivates teachers? Student achievement, lessons they can do tomorrow, and materials to do those lessons with. Money motivates some, but not for the best reasons. We could have taken those values and blended them with research on student learning in mathematics. We should have promised teachers that if they participated in project events, their students would learn more. Instead we relied on intrinsic interest. That was enough to motivate some, but not everyone. We should have focused our attention on student understanding. We could still have provided access to manipulatives, calculators, and lessons to do tomorrow, but we could have sharpened them with more content and pedagogy.

The MIE project was at a disadvantage because the schools had made so many other major professional development commitments, including a major literacy project, revamping behavioral management plans, and extending the science program. How could we add such an ambitious new project? The funding iron was hot, so we struck. It would have been interesting to start slower and worked intensively with several volunteer teachers and MSU faculty members to develop teacher leaders in mathematics. Starting with a select group of teachers and faculty would have given the project time to develop classrooms—in both the university and the schools—that modeled and encouraged the types of teaching we were after.

3

Negotiating Borders

The primary mission of any college of education is to prepare educators for the complex world of schooling, teaching, and learning. In order to become effective educators, preservice students must have consistent and coherent experiences in schools and at the university. Preservice education, the intersection between the university and the schools, was a cornerstone of the MIE project. The MIE project leaders had a vision of simultaneous renewal, which requires a systems approach and the concurrent improvement of preservice, inservice, and university education.

Our vision for preservice students was fourfold:

- We wanted them to have an exemplary experience in mathematics education so they'd leave the program as mathematically competent teachers.
- We wanted them to be comfortable, competent, and experienced in elementary classrooms, with a rich set of field experiences that would give them a high level of comfort and ability as teachers.
- We wanted them to be able to bridge their university experiences with their classroom experiences through reflection and application. This would help them develop reflective and critical faculties.
- We wanted the students in the project to possess or be able to acquire analytic abilities and strong academic preparation to do the work we expected them to do in their classrooms.

Where would our student participants come from?

The first questions Karen and I had were about selecting students to participate in MIE. Should we try to recruit mathematics enthusiasts? That would make our lives easier: If students came to the project with a decent understanding and appreciation of mathematics we could concentrate on making them proficient teachers. But there was a counterargument: What would it prove if we took only students who were already strong in mathematics and made them stronger? The mathematics background knowledge of the typical elementary education major isn't as rich and strong as many believe it should be. If we took strong students, the project would not be easy to replicate because there aren't large numbers of elementary preservice teachers who are particularly strong in mathematics. Ultimately, we decided to select students according to the LiC program guidelines. While they had slightly higher grade point averages (GPAs) than other MSU education students overall, our cohort was fairly average in terms of their mathematics preparation. Several students liked mathematics and did well in it. A handful had taken calculus. Their entering surveys revealed that most seemed to appreciate mathematics. A couple feared it. We knew that if we could start with this fairly representative sample of the student population and turn them into skilled mathematics teachers, the MIE project would have more credibility than if we started with students who were already strong in mathematics content knowledge. We developed the students' courses and experiences keeping in mind that we had a group with average abilities and interests in mathematics.

Most students who applied understood that LiC was different from the regular program at the university. It involved dramatically more field experiences. Courses in some semesters were blocked, thus making it difficult or impossible for the students to take other courses. The students had to commit to a three-year program that had almost no flexibility. They had to apply in the spring before their sophomore year, so they had to be organized and certain about their plans. Applicants were screened by the prospective partner schools and by LiC administrators. They were selected based on GPAs, an application letter, and their reports about any previous experiences they had had in school-like settings.

This selection process and the structure of the program led to an unintended outcome: The students were relatively homogeneous. Of twenty-four students, all but two were white. There were only three male students. Most students were nineteen or twenty. It seemed at times that the cohort was full of young, blond Emilys. One student, Jamal, singlehandedly diversified the cohort. He was male, in his mid-twenties, and African American. Older students may have had a difficult time committing to the extra field experiences in the schools and the evening cohort meetings

44

that the program required. Family and financial constraints also restricted the range of people who could commit. The program encouraged applications from both elementary and secondary education students, but ultimately all but one were elementary majors. Secondary education students had a difficult time completing their major content courses within the scheduling constraints of the LiC structure. Of the twenty-four students who started with the cohort, twenty-one finished the program. Those who left included the two African American students. One quit because of family needs. People who had outside responsibilities like families and jobs had a hard time making space in their day for the extra commitments. People who were different were outsiders—a difficult position to handle for three years.

I regularly had students in other methods courses who were slightly off beat. Most classes included someone who was older and returning to school. A single parent struggling to keep a job and keep up with classes. Someone changing careers. Or a middle-aged parent returning to college with her kids, fulfilling a dream deferred. Take Doug, for example. He was in his early forties. He worked in retail for years but had always wanted to be a teacher. Now that his kids were in high school, he decided the time was right to switch careers. Eventually, he found himself in my science methods course. Doug brought a passion for midwest frontier history to our class. On Halloween, he arrived in class dressed head to foot in beaded buckskins, with long fringe blowing in the gusty October wind. He was an impressive sight made even more remarkable by the fact he had killed and skinned the deer, tanned the hide, created the beadwork, and sewed the clothes all with implements of the early nineteenth century. The young students in our class seemed slightly embarrassed by this spectacle. But I still have the bison molar and porcupine quills that Doug collected for me. He would not have fit in with our cohort of young, ambitious undergraduates. This was sad for two reasons: It deprived Doug of the special opportunities available in LiC and it deprived the cohort students of his knowledge, passion, and maturity.

Preparation in Mathematics

The primary motivation behind funding the MIE project was an interest in mathematics education in elementary schools. Everything

Karen and I did for the project had a grounding in mathematics. But elementary teachers are, virtually by definition, generalists, and their undergraduate courses reflect this. They take a little math, science, history, PE, art, and music. The MSU students' program was already packed, so adding more mathematics courses was unrealistic. How would we make this a mathematics-flavored cohort? The only option was to integrate mathematics into the students' existing coursework, which we thought would be easy enough. Faculty members could be encouraged by project funds to tweak their courses by adding or developing connections to mathematics. This encouragement could take the form of extra technology (such as a new computer) and money to travel to professional meetings. How hard could it be to create a mathematics-based cohort? And what would it look like?

Integrating Mathematics into University Coursework

One of the project's objectives was to make certain that university education students would have positive attitudes about mathematics by the time they graduated. Obviously, this meant that some attitudes would be maintained, some changed, and some created. We know that mathematics attitudes and mathematics achievement are linked. Whether or not there is a causal relationship is difficult to document, but attitude and achievement seem to travel together. We intended that project students would become aware of the mathematics in everyday life. This would force them to rethink the idea that mathematics was an isolated academic subject. They would experience mathematics in real contexts in their own university courses. We expected that as they learned more mathematics, their attitudes would be enhanced as they saw mathematics in meaningful contexts. This synergy would propel them to a new understanding of learning and teaching mathematics.

Assuming that connecting mathematics to real life would give students a more robust appreciation and understanding of mathematics, Karen and I set to work looking for opportunities to study mathematics in the undergraduate curriculum. We started with the university coursework. How could professors integrate mathematics into their lessons? Perhaps they could discuss the ways in which statistics have been used to describe different student populations. If a professor used a bar graph, she could discuss the generation of the graph and its implications for communicating ideas. When they learned that millions of U.S. students spend more hours in a day watching TV than attending school, students could briefly discuss conceptions of large numbers: "Just how large is one million, anyhow?" Students might become aware of how the use of numbers affects individuals or groups. How have SAT scores or IQ tests been used to create or deny opportunities? Karen and I provided the professor of the education program's foundations course (which addresses the cultural, historical, and political dimensions of schools) with an elementary mathematics curriculum centered on social issues. Preservice students would learn how social issues could serve as a context for learning mathematics. These were Karen's visions for integrating mathematics into the students' undergraduate curriculum before the students' methods semester. These sorts of experiences would distinguish them from other LiC groups.

Ultimately, the effort to integrate mathematics into the university curriculum was disappointing. The university courses for the MIE cohort (for reasons explored in Chapter 4) were no different from those taught in the regular education program. This made the mathematics focus less than obvious for the preservice students in the first year and a half of the project.

Mega-Methods

The most distinctive course of the LiC program was a mega-methods course that combined methods courses in reading, social studies, science, and mathematics. Course time during mega-methods was compressed. The usual sixteen-week semester was only ten weeks in mega-methods because the students were in elementary school classrooms for the other six weeks. The intention was to integrate the content and field experiences of the four methods courses. While there were still four separate instructors, each with the responsibility for one course, the courses were connected as much as possible.

Karen and Camille, a social studies methods instructor, had taught previous mega-methods courses. The two new faculty recruits were Rita, a reading methods instructor, and me. I would teach science methods. Karen and Camille warned us about the time commitment, and they were right. Teaching a mega-methods course dropped us into a black hole of meetings. We had to share with others about how and what we taught, a rare occurrence at the university level. Then we had to align what we taught and find things in common. This should serve as a warning to anyone who intends to plan an integrated curriculum: It takes a considerable commitment of time, a willingness to compromise, and a serious evaluation of what's being taught. We four had considerable dissension. Rita admitted that she didn't particularly care about the cohort, mathematics, or the MIE project. Her one and only agenda, an imposing one at that, was to teach her students how to teach reading, period. I admired her focus and determination, but for this project we needed mathematics to share center stage. We could work it out, though, because mathematics is everywhere—right?

So we talked and we tweaked our classes and we talked some more. We came up with some threads to teach. Then we moved to the specifics. This turned out to be much more cumbersome than I had ever imagined. Students would write a lesson plan in any of our subjects but would have to write a companion lesson for mathematics. The undergraduates also had to connect a lesson in mathematics with one in science, social studies, or reading. This practice placated Rita, who didn't want to lose any of her regular reading assignments. I graded the science lessons, Rita covered reading, and Camille looked at social studies. Karen read all of the mathematics connections. None of us wanted to grade papers outside our area of expertise. Ironically, while we were requiring students to make connections, we weren't comfortable doing it ourselves.

That sounds discouraging. If it had ended there, it would have been. But we learned lessons to help us in the future. The primary lesson was that there should be intensive professional development of faculty before they attempt this type of mega-methods activity. The first priority should be for instructors to be comfortable and competent with the content areas before committing much time in class to integrating the areas. The second lesson was that thoughtful content integration takes time. If we wanted students or faculty to devote attention to content integration, they must both understand the content and have time to devote to aligning and, if appropriate, blending the content areas. Another instructional focus, like breadth of coverage, might have to go. In this age of new standards and increasing accountability, we keep piling new obligations onto both preservice and inservice teachers—then we wonder why nothing is done very well. To help students make connections between content areas, we need to provide time, and time is scarce in both schools and universities.

Action Research

Following their mega-methods semester, the MIE students took one other class that wasn't available to students in the regular program, a class in action research. This class required that the students develop a research question and protocol, then conduct the research in a classroom. The project leaders hoped that this class would help students put all of the pieces together—practice with theory. In many ways, this happened. Most of the projects were quite thoughtful. Molly investigated the effects of music on spatial reasoning skills in a second-grade classroom. Emily and Christy, both of whom worked on certification in elementary math, examined the effects of journal writing on fourth and fifth graders' understanding of fractions. One group investigated the effects of the introduction of an animal into a second-grade room. Another looked at the motivational effects of technology programs in middle school reading. One project was on gender differences in recess behavior; another looked at desk configurations and the classroom behavior and achievement of fourth-grade students. They were all interesting, and covered the gamut of classroom issues: behavior, recess, content knowledge, computer use.

The students presented their findings at the end of the semester. Faculty from MSU's Department of Curriculum and Instruction were invited. The presentations were an enormous success. These were the most powerful action research projects in the five years of the LiC program. Camille, the instructor, was justifiably proud—but Lincoln and Forest teachers were not. The course became a sore point. I had made a deliberate request that the students present their findings to the faculties at Lincoln and Forest, for two reasons. First, this project represented a collaboration between the schools and the university. It blended the research focus of the university with practice at the schools. It was a perfect opportunity to showcase to the university, the schools, and the undergraduates what collaboration could look like and provide.

Second, getting teachers interested in participating had proven to be difficult. I had to do a lot of behind-the-scenes marketing to get teachers to sign on. They knew what practica were, and they supported the idea of preservice teachers practicing their teaching. But "action research"? What was *that?* The teachers weren't sure what value the course would have to their classrooms or to the preservice teachers. I promised them that the project would not be disruptive and the students would present their results. But for reasons of university and student convenience, the presentations were done at a time when the classroom teachers could not attend. The students had a hard time finding space in their schedule to present at the schools, so the Lincoln-Forest teachers never really saw the presentations. At my request, one group agreed to talk about their project at a faculty meeting in January. They gave a quick two-minute, ad libbed presentation to the teachers, nothing like their polished presentations to the faculty. Instead of showing the potential of action research to the teachers, these students made it look like little more was involved than sharing hunches. In the end, the course had little meaning to the teachers, who just saw it as another hoop for the students to jump through.

The class would have had more power if the students had worked more with teachers to develop researchable questions whose answers could help the teachers teach better. In this way, both teachers and students would have benefited. But the logistical problems of having a full schedule and an unclear notion of the value of the course led students to work independently of the teachers. I still found promise, though, in the sophistication of their projects. Had they only consulted more with the classroom teachers, the class would have been even more productive.

The emphasis on mathematics, even if it wasn't as smooth or as consistent as we might have liked, did establish the MIE students as a mathematics cohort. Although some students complained about the MSU faculty and vice versa, in the end it was also a bonding experience. After a summer's rest and time to reflect, the undergraduates came back in the fall citing the enormous growth they had experienced in the semester. It was like boot camp—you hate it while going through it but credit it as a life-changing experience once you are done.

The Power of Informal Experiences

The project funds provided a variety of other opportunities that would affect the preparation of the preservice students to teach mathematics. These experiences set this student cohort apart from the regular MSU education program as well as from previous LiC cohorts. For example, the three student project leaders attended an annual conference of K–3 mathematics specialists along with university and school leaders. They met elementary teachers, leaders, and researchers from around the country who were catalysts in the booming mathematics education reform movement. These students were gregarious and curious. They asked questions and participated. The other members of the group included them and appreciated their enthusiasm. Rubbing elbows with people like Ruth Parker and Constance Kamii gave the students the thrill of belonging to an important movement. The experience was an induction into their profession. They saw how seriously and passionately the subject was treated, they valued the respect given to them by other attendees, and they converted to the math reform effort.

Two of the most dramatic experiences the larger group of students had were attending the annual NCTM conference on two occasions. During their sophomore year, not even a year into their program, the students received enough money from the foundation and MSU to cover their transportation, hotel, and registration for a conference. This was an incredible opportunity. While the students appreciated it, they didn't fully understand its implications. The national meeting is daunting even for experienced teachers. How do you choose sessions? What sense do you make out of what you hear and do? How can you apply what you learn? While the students didn't know enough yet to make sense of the meeting, they did know that it was special and that they were privileged to attend.

The following year's conference was even more influential. Not only did the students know how to get more out of the conference, they presented. A large group of students created a presentation about communication. Others developed posters they presented. In the year between the two conferences they had developed some criteria and strategies for choosing events. From their work in the schools and in their mathematics methods course, they knew what types of sessions would be interesting and helpful to them. One pair of students was excited about a session in which they used tangrams to develop spatial thinking skills. The previous year, they hadn't known what tangrams were. The students had grown in that year from having a sense of importance about attending the conference to having a better understanding of how the meetings provided them with professional development. They were developing an emerging sense of professionalism.

Another informal experience that contributed to the growth of the students in the math-focused cohort was making contributions to the monthly MIE newsletter that went to teachers, administrators, and university faculty. Each month different MSU students were expected to find examples of the NCTM standards in action and write a brief piece for the newsletter. This heightened their awareness of math in the classroom and also made them much more familiar with the standards.

At the end of student teaching, almost all of the preservice students reported that they had learned more math and had an even better attitude about it. Where did this growth come from? I suspect it came from their experiences with attendance at the NCTM conferences, their participation in writing a monthly MIE newsletter, and the mathematics focus in their methods courses.

Focusing on Mathematics in the Classroom

The mathematics focus of the preservice students would have been difficult to maintain without a similar focus on the part of the classroom teachers and the schools. Everywhere the university students turned they saw a focus on math. When the Lincoln art teacher taught second graders about Picasso, our university students saw geometry. They saw math in science lessons about the seasons. They noticed that a first-grade teacher doing a lesson on reading a map was also teaching discrete math. Together with their methods class assignment to connect math lessons to other content areas, seeing this focus in the classroom cemented their ideas about mathematics as an animated subject that is important beyond the fifty-minute class period.

The students also saw that well over half of the classroom teachers participated in professional development activities in math. Teachers attended the math miniconferences the schools hosted and were able to order math supplies and attend activities such as Marilyn Burns or TI calculator workshops. Most teachers supported their assigned undergraduates as they tried new ways of math teaching.

I have visited other universities with content-focused preservice programs. In talking with students in these programs it's become clear to me that if the schools don't buy in to the program as much as the university does, the advantage of focusing on content is lost and frustration sets in. Preservice students in science cohorts, assigned to a school that doesn't emphasize science, cannot practice what they learned in their university courses. The MIE project was able to avoid that kind of disconnect. Through a mix of coursework, classroom practice, and other opportunities, the preservice teachers graduated with a heightened view of their abilities to teach mathematics. They learned some math, learned ways to teach it, and practiced in classrooms where there was support. The combination of the mathematics focus with extended classroom experiences gave them more confidence as they headed into their own classrooms.

Preparation for Teaching

Preservice students understand long before they ever set foot in a classroom as the teacher that more classroom experience will make them better teachers. If you ask teachers where they learned to teach, they start with their experiences in schools, not with their methods or foundations courses. Most experienced teachers cite their student-teaching experience as the most potent learning experience they had in their preservice program. If you are going to teach, you need practice.

Yet we all know teachers who have twenty or thirty years of practice but who are not, by our standards, good teachers. Experience itself isn't the only teacher. Experience can be more powerful when it's considered through a lens of reflection, theory, and research. Our challenge in the MIE project was to respect classroom teachers' experience and provide extensive opportunities for preservice students to practice teaching, yet keep them open to different ways of teaching and learning. Experience for its own sake wasn't the goal. We wanted students to extend the meaning of their experience to include the perspectives of others, research, and accepted pedagogical practice. In short, we wanted to blend the university side with the school side.

Planning and Scheduling Classroom Assignments

Realizing this vision of a mathematics learning community required classroom teachers who could model careful and appropriate mathematics instruction. These would be teachers who sought out professional development experiences for themselves. We want high-quality mentors for any university student just as we want high-quality teachers for our children. But the reality too often does not meet that goal. Teachers have different strengths. Some may like language arts but not teach mathematics well. The MIE project gave us the excuse to favor those who were strong in mathematics teaching. We had money and the authority of the foundation behind us. Yet we soon found out that all the money and outside authority in the world cannot, by itself, change the culture of a school.

We quickly lost control of university students' classroom placements. I was originally asked to place students for the practica, but that presented a delicate problem. I was a teacher at Lincoln. In the school's culture, all teachers are created equal. My assigning the students created a power imbalance. The other teachers didn't want a colleague making public judgments about them, and they didn't want to compete with each other for preservice students. The teachers wanted the principals to make the call. The principals chose teachers to participate in this project as they would choose them for any practicum. Some teachers were selected because they were good math teachers. Other teachers were simply available. A couple had university students placed in their rooms for political reasons or to keep them happy. The placements for the MIE practica became as haphazard as any other placements.

I still struggle with this question. Do you limit participation to those teachers who can model professional behaviors consistent with national standards? If you do, the pool may be small and the politics of selection delicate. Do you place preservice students wherever someone will take them? That avoids favoritism or elitism, but it creates another dilemma: The teacher may not model effective teaching or allow the student to practice other ways of teaching. Given the choice, I would opt for teachers who are competent and flexible, even at the risk of offending others.

Off to a Shaky Start

The LiC program provided the structure for the extended set of field experiences. Each semester in the three-year sequence had some sort of practicum. The practicum in the first semester was purely exploratory. Students briefly observed in three schools: a high school, an elementary school, and a middle school. They had no teaching assignments. They never became attached to a school, much less a classroom. It was, the students thought, a good way to sample a variety of schools.

The teachers at Lincoln and Forest were disappointed, however. The arrival of the university students had been built up so successfully that teachers were eager to work with them. Karen and I had explained that in these three years the students would become part of our staff. Preservice students would have such extensive contact with the classrooms that it would be like having additional teachers. Then the students arrived, made a few quick visits, and disappeared. The teachers wondered, quite loudly, where this extensive contact was taking place. It was difficult to explain that the program was designed to give students a broad perspective before assigning them to one school. As the school-based MIE representative, I heard an earful. I tried to explain that the students would eventually come back to spend a large chunk of time at our schools. This placated the teachers, but it was clear that they should have been better informed about the structure and logic behind the program.

I still smile when I think of the students' first visit to Lincoln. A fellow teacher took my class so I could greet them. The students arrived a little early—a good sign. They walked through the front doors in a large clump as if they were being herded by invisible Shelties. They looked well scrubbed, dressed up, and nervous, like an elementary class on the first day of school. I treated them the way I would treat other "new kids." I wanted to protect them, show off the school, and make them want to come back. We covered the typical school landmarks: Here's the nurse's office. The cafeteria. The library. The ever-important rest rooms. Through the semester, as the students returned a few more times, they began to wear their khakis more often than their dress-up clothes, and they seemed visibly more relaxed.

In the next semester, the teachers and university students started to get to know each other better. The students became slightly more visible in the schools. They stayed in the same classroom and even taught a lesson or two to satisfy the requirements of a general methods course. Unfortunately, these first steps toward building a university presence in the schools was followed by a semester in which students weren't assigned to the schools. Instead, their professor in multicultural education expected them to interview social services agency representatives from the neighborhood. That was a valuable experience for the students, but it meant that they were once again phantoms to Lincoln-Forest teachers.

The Tide Turns . . . Temporarily

University student involvement in the schools continued to be inconsistent through the first three semesters of the project. The fourth semester, when the students took the mega-methods class, changed the landscape. Just as the mega-methods semester was a watershed event for the university, it was also important for the relationships among the university students and the teachers. The preservice students were in the classroom for six full weeks. They had a virtual student-teaching experience. The elementary students saw the preservice teachers as assistant teachers in the classroom. The elementary teachers saw them as student teachers. The preservice students attended faculty meetings—or were supposed to, anyway. They were beginning to feel like teachers. Their journals and interviews revealed that they were developing proprietary feelings: The students talked about "my teacher," "my classroom," and "my students." The preservice teachers had become, with only a few exceptions, comfortable in the schools. As a new relationship developed between the preservice teachers and their mentor teachers, the mentors saw the university students grow considerably and the preservice students got a taste of being a "real" teacher. They started to identify themselves as teachers rather than as students.

In the last semester before student teaching, the university students took their action research course. Most, but not all, spent some time in a classroom, but it was nothing compared to the time spent in the mega-methods semester. Students did a variety of things. Some observed playground behavior. One administered a survey. But they taught no lessons and did no formal, sustained work. Then they were gone.

This ebb and flow of the field experiences proved to be difficult for both the university students and the teachers. The students were here, were gone, were at the schools consistently, then disappeared again. The teachers found it frustrating because their students left just as soon as they got to know them. A teacher might never see a student again. The students were frustrated because just as they got comfortable, learned the routines, and started feeling like teachers, they had to leave. The LiC program created this staccato structure of field experiences based on the requirements of the mega-methods and action research courses. The structure worked well for the university, but it didn't work well for the university students, the schools, or the relationship between the schools and the university. The flow of the students' experiences should have been more obvious and consistent to the students.

The extended field experiences did make most students more comfortable in the schools and helped them clarify what they wanted in their careers. Some had never thought about working in an inner-city school before their work at Lincoln-Forest. By the end of that work, several felt compelled to stay in urban settings, which made them feel needed. Others confirmed their preference for small rural schools. Some were surprised to find that they were interested in middle schools. As the students sampled an array of grades and subjects, their goals became more clear. The intense experiences in schools supported students who felt a little shy. In the regular program they might have struggled in student teaching or in their first year of teaching. But in this program they got so much experience that they grew more comfortable than they could have without it. In one case, the experience had a surprising result: A student realized that teaching was not for her. While that was a painful conclusion, it was better for her to find it out in the low-risk atmosphere of being a student than in the high-risk environment of a first-year teacher, when so many people would have depended on her. With so much time in the schools, everyone came to better understand their strengths, preferences, and needs.

Lessons Learned

Placements Students will learn from their experiences in classrooms. That's the good news. It's also the bad news. If the placement isn't consistent with the program's message, preservice
students will align with what they view as "real"—what they have
seen in the classroom. If a classroom teacher believes that children must memorize the multiplication table before they attempt
to solve a problem, the preservice teacher is likely to think that
belief has merit. Placements should be based on the fit between
the student, the teacher, and the university. But even in the best
of programs, placements must be based on politics, "fairness," logistics, and any number of other reasons. The key is to offer the
student and teacher the support and interactions necessary so that
the student grows in a desirable direction. Debrief with the student often. Observe frequently. Even offer to guest teach. Much
good can come from a weak placement, but only if it is planned.

Timing Karen and I thought the project's increased hours of field
experience leading up to student teaching would bond the university students with Lincoln-Forest. We were wrong. About half
of the students chose other options for their student teaching.
Some went out of state, where job prospects were better. A few
took opportunities to teach overseas in Czechoslovakia and New
Zealand—exotic places for mostly rural midwesterners. Almost
half of the students weren't ready to student teach in the planned
semester. Because of the requirements of the program, students
hadn't been able to work on their university requirements in their
minors and general education. As a result, only a few student
taught at Lincoln or Forest. This made some of the classroom
teachers bitter. Some had really wanted to continue the relationship with the student they had in mega-methods. Others never
got a student but wanted one. "Can I have Craig?" No, he went to
New Mexico. "Can I have Suzie?" No, she went to New Zealand.
"Rachel?" Sorry, Omaha got her.

  While it may have created difficulties with the students, we
should have limited their choices for student teaching to Lincoln
or Forest. The teachers had invested much of their time and emo-
tion in the MIE students and they expected that student teaching

was where their investment would pay off. The preservice students would be able to contribute to the classroom and be more independent. They would anticipate more needs in the classroom and serve as a coteacher rather than as an apprentice. I believe that the students owed a debt to the partner schools and should have completed their university experience there. The students might also have profited from sticking together. They had spent two and a half years together, then suddenly, in the culminating experience, they split up. They no longer had each other's support.

Supervision There is nothing more important to a preservice teacher than student teaching. This is where their preparation can be translated to practice. But it's commonly recognized that colleges of education don't place the same value on student teaching. Who supervises student teachers—faculty members? Not usually. The task is commonly left to adjuncts, often retired principals or teachers, or to graduate assistants. These people may not share or even be aware of the university's values. This practice inadvertently reinforces the notion that students' university work isn't connected to their lives as teachers. That's exactly the wrong message for them to get.

Teacher Involvement If classroom teachers are expected to value and participate in educating preservice teachers, they need to be given a voice. Classroom assignments should be made with their input. If they failed to respond to surveys, ask a different way. At the very least, arrange to include them in debriefings with the student.

Involve Other Preservice Students Teaching is often shared only between the teacher and the students. Teachers don't usually open their classrooms to each other, much less to university outsiders. Isolationism permeates school culture. How can we break this pattern? One way would be to introduce preservice teachers to the benefits of peer observation. If we made observation part of the regular education program in a way that benefited students, students would learn the value of collaboration and cooperation among peers.

These lessons are not new. Other projects and studies have reported the same conclusions. The point is that simply changing the structure of teacher education, such as by increasing field experiences, necessarily change what preservice teachers learn. Attention needs to be paid to how program structures can be used to support quality reflective practice.

Bridging University and Practice

A goal for MIE was to connect the undergraduates' university and school experiences. The participation of university faculty members was critical on several fronts. First, we needed them to make mathematics connections in their courses. Second, in order for the preservice students to connect their university and field experiences, faculty members needed to be involved in the schools themselves.

Unfortunately, most of the faculty involved in the project didn't connect mathematics to their coursework despite being given new computers or other incentives. Faculty involvement in the schools was also limited. Karen spent most of her time in a few classrooms at Forest, only going to Lincoln when invited.

The consequence of this lack of faculty involvement was that the preservice students didn't have the opportunity to bridge the two worlds. Like any other preservice students they lived double lives: They had their university coursework. They had their school experiences. Opportunities to blend the two were limited because the students would have had to make the connections on their own, and it's unlikely that novice teachers would be able to do that.

The increase in field experiences did have positive effects on the preservice students. They became familiar with school routines and developed a much greater level of confidence in the classroom than did students in the regular program. Over and over again the preservice students listed their time in schools as the most powerful part of their three years. This wasn't without drawbacks. The students started to resist their coursework. As emerging experts in the classroom, they judged their university work to be irrelevant. They saw the class on action research as a distraction—real teachers don't do research. The university students were champing at the bit to be "real" teachers. Their mega-methods semester was so intense that the next two semesters, even student teaching, seemed like an annoyance. They were ready to teach. They felt competent.

This is a problem in most teacher education programs. The college work is seen as theoretical and the classroom as where real knowledge is constructed. Potential remedies for this condition abound, but the answers aren't clear. How can we educate future teachers to continue to improve by learning from both their classroom experiences and the research literature? We can force them to do it while they're students, but once they're teaching, how can learning and reflection continue to develop? There are clear ways not to bridge the gap between the university and the schools. Expanding field experiences leads to more comfortable students, but does it make them better teachers? Not unless the messages from the university and school sides are consistent. With the MIE project, we hoped that there would be more cooperation between the schools and the university, but distance and time conspired against it. The faculty had no time to drive forty miles to meet with teachers and observe students. The teachers were even less able to visit the university. The result was that the preservice students saw little interaction between the classroom teachers and the university instructors. The exercises in making connections became superficial.

Collaboration with Classroom Teachers

Karen and I wanted to make sure that the undergraduate students saw us in the schools and saw us working with the Lincoln-Forest teachers. We brainstormed some ideas and decided to take our university show on the road. We enlisted Anna, who was teaching a combined first- and second-grade class at Lincoln, to work with us. We intended for the undergraduates to be actively involved as well. The lesson we did connected the science curriculum on light and shadows with the mathematics curriculum on spatial reasoning. Groups of children were to work with pairs of undergraduates. The undergraduates would use stacking wooden cubes to build a simple structure with a pattern. The elementary students would try to discover the pattern and then extend it. We also asked the elementary students to predict what the shadow of the structure would look like if a flashlight were directed at it from above. The lesson seemed to go well. The elementary students were engaged and curious. The undergraduates for the most part actively tried to engage their groups of students. Some struggled but still succeeded in asking good questions. A few succumbed to the temptation to do the work themselves as the elementary students just watched. Karen, Anna, and I worked our way around the room, observing and helping.

After the children left, we discussed the lesson with the preservice students. Karen and I had planned to talk about questioning strategies, but the students were obsessed with classroom management issues. They diverted every question we asked. How do you keep a wiggly kid on task? What if a child dominates the group? How do you keep blocks from becoming projectiles? These questions were all addressed to Anna. Karen and I faded into the scenery. It was as if the lesson had been taught purely for the purpose of keeping kids on task. In our discussion afterward, Karen expressed disappointment but not surprise. Preservice teachers often focus on behavior management. The prospect of "losing control" seems to be a recurrent nightmare for preservice teachers. I wondered if the undergraduates didn't understand the reason for the lesson. Karen assured me that it could be the most simple, obvious lesson in the world and preservice teachers would still worry about keeping Dwayne in his seat and making Nicole keep her hands to herself. Those things are important, but focusing on management alone leaves out other things, like models of instruction and content. It even precludes examining the relationship between the task and student behavior.

Karen and I should have been more thoughtful and included Anna in our planning, developing our purpose for the lesson in common. Anna couldn't possibly have known what we wanted the students to focus on, so it was natural for her to go with what the students noticed—management problems. It was good that Karen and I were in the schools and teaching, but it would have been better if we had included the classroom teacher.

The Dilemmas of Supervision

LiC had a built-in structure to encourage university–school connections: Each cohort had a site coordinator to coordinate and supervise the students' field experiences and to serve as the university's representative in the schools. The site coordinator was expected to know the schools and be known in the schools. But who should this person be? Work in schools is so time-consuming that untenured faculty members were justifiably wary of the job. Across the country, junior faculty are warned against working in schools. The amount of time needed jeopardizes their chance for tenure unless the university itself values the time. Unfortunately, many university departments, even in colleges of education, don't value work done in schools.

If there was a site coordinator for the first year of the MIE project, I don't know who it was. The teachers weren't aware of a site coordinator. There were no MSU faculty members at the school except those who attended after-school meetings. Technically Amy may have been the coordinator, because the undergraduates recognized her as their university connection. She led some pizza-laden evening meetings in the first year. But most teachers, unless they came to planning meetings, didn't know Amy, who never went into classrooms. Whoever the site coordinator may have been, connections between the university and the school were not being made.

Lisa was made site coordinator in the project's second year. The choice was unfair to her and to the project. She was a first-year professor without any university or school teaching experience or interest in mathematics education. She volunteered time in Cindy's class and tutored some fourth graders, but she was unknown to the undergraduates. In the massive mega-methods semester she was invisible. Students didn't know her. Most teachers didn't know her. Many teachers assumed that Karen or I was the site coordinator. Both of us took on some of those responsibilities out of loyalty to the project. But we were also sensitive to the perils of assuming too much authority where we technically had none.

The supervision of mega-methods had more potential to establish a university presence at the schools. I was at Lincoln as a staff member, and the three other MSU faculty members observed student lessons as part of their commitment to mega-methods. Each faculty member was at a school three or four times during the semester. For the university, this was a massive change. The course was a huge time commitment for instructors. We got no extra credit for our teaching load and the schools were forty miles apart. The faculty members considered their involvement a service beyond the usual scope of teaching a course. The great expectations held by both teachers and students soured some of this achievement. Even though it was unheard of for faculty to supervise pre–student teaching field experiences, both university students and teachers were expecting something different. Karen and I had built the expectation of community, and a brief observation followed by a long car ride back to the university was not what the teachers or students envisioned. The students and teachers expected faculty to be there more. The faculty felt they were already donating enough time. It was a no-win situation.

The supervision of mega-methods turned out to be the highlight of university supervision. In the following semester, in which students did action research projects, there was no university faculty presence in the schools. Supervision of student teaching reverted to the usual practice of hiring retired teachers and principals. These people were competent, but they had no knowledge of the university courses or of MIE. The students' field experiences were disconnected from their university experience. That disconnection was antithetical to the goals of the project. But unless the university's values and expectations changed, the inconsistencies between students' experiences would remain.

Teacher Participation in Supervision

The goals of the project, at least with respect to student supervision, were also difficult to negotiate with school culture at Lincoln and Forest. Karen and I planned for teachers to take a more active role in student supervision, but the teachers had no time or interest in doing so. As they saw it, supervision was the university's job. On several occasions university faculty asked teachers for suggestions or input about assignments. The only person who got such input was a former Lincoln teacher, Jane, who taught a reading methods course to the MIE cohort. She was barraged by suggestions. Perhaps the teachers responded to her because they saw her as a colleague. Perhaps they were more comfortable offering suggestions about teaching reading than about teaching mathematics or social studies. These teachers chose to be elementary teachers. They wanted to see more university faculty at the schools but they had no desire to do what they viewed as university work.

Cohort Issues

Peer Support

As the students in the project matured, they learned to support each other, forming cliques that gave them support and a sense of safety and protection—sometimes from the other cliques. Groups of students worked together and some even socialized together. They shared rides to school and traded stories of engagement rings, vacation surprises, and the other mysteries of being young. They helped make the large university program feel more personal for one another.

The cliques weren't always positive. They bickered constantly in the beginning. But despite their difficulties, students solicited cohort opinions, and in a final evaluation they reported that the cohort was one of the strongest elements in their preservice program. They had learned, sometimes kicking and screaming, to work in a group. While part of this growth was due to growing up (they came to the project as teenagers and left as young professionals), it also had to do with paying active attention to working together. The students met monthly, traveled together to NCTM meetings, and saw each other constantly in university courses. At times they got sick of each other or angry, but they learned to work it out or get over it.

Faculty Leadership of Cohort Interactions

Most of the cohort students were about twenty. Many celebrated their twenty-first birthdays together. I thought of these young people as adults, and they were. But they were also transitioning from adolescence into young adulthood. They were not, for the most part, mature adults. The students were assembled into a cohort without much attention to how they should work together. The goal from the faculty side was to get students to share experiences and support each other. The goal from the student side was never articulated.

The students, spending most of their work hours together, developed their own social organization. The results weren't always very pretty. Without more mature leadership some of the less pleasant aspects of high school returned. They developed their own social organization that wasn't supportive. The negative students were few in number—not more than a handful. But through intimidation they were able to control the tone of the cohort. At first the other students were afraid of them, but as the students matured and grew in their confidence, they were less likely to give the few negative students much power.

This negative aspect to cohort membership could have been tempered with more faculty involvement. While faculty were assigned to teach classes, no one was designated to nurture the social development of the cohort. In the cohort that followed this one, a faculty member was assigned who spent a lot of time with the group. As a result, the students were aware of the goals for the cohort and guided to a positive disposition. They still had conflicts, but the conflicts became opportunities to learn, not blame.

Student Leadership

The MIE cohort was selected through the input of Lincoln and Forest teachers and through review at the university. Together, teachers and faculty chose students who seemed a little better prepared academically than the average elementary education student. In their first quarter as a cohort, they elected three students to represent them in meetings with faculty and administrators. These three students learned, at times painfully, the responsibilities and the headaches of leadership. If they made a decision that was unpopular they were called bullies. If they failed to make a decision they were considered ineffective. After their first year, the student leaders were battle scarred. They thought about quitting, but they persevered. Their fellow students reelected them for two more years. The cohort students gradually learned how to provide input for decision making, and in the end they gave the student leaders some positive recognition. The leaders learned how to solicit more opinions, compromise, and communicate more effectively. In short, all the students grew up.

Elitism

Through focus group interviews and other observations, it was clear that the cohort had created a club that didn't value outside opinion. They considered the university an "outsider." They sought out each other's opinions about classroom situations, considering their cohort colleagues as experts. They gave each other advice on classes, teaching, and getting a job. They might consider a class-room teacher's advice, but they actively dismissed or distrusted in-formation from the university. In focus groups they blasted their university classes and many of their professors.

Values

The implementation of the MIE project was linked to such issues as supervision and coursework, the structure and purpose of which will greatly affect any project as broad as this one. But structural issues and program elements like the cohort need to be seen in a broader context. Any attempt to effect lasting change in educa-tion must consider the values held by the stakeholders. If reform efforts contradict deeply held values, they are unlikely to succeed. We found that the preservice teachers had values that overlapped with many, but not all, of the teachers' values, and that differed distinctly from those held at the university. Their values con-stantly filtered what the students were able to learn and do. At some points their values were a catalyst for positive changes. At other times, their values interfered with connections Karen and I had hoped would be made.

The university students' strongest value was in their apprecia-tion for the importance of their elementary school students. They deeply cared, as do most practicing teachers, about the children's attitudes and achievement. They hoped with a very deep convic-tion that they could make a difference in children's lives. They wanted their classrooms to be joyous places that inspired children to learn. Their children would be happy, helpful, and friendly. They would be so overcome with the riches of the classroom that they would be determined to be lifelong learners. Did the univer-sity students care that their students enjoy and achieve in mathe-matics in particular? Sure, they all did. A few wanted to share their love of mathematics. Several wanted to save their students from experiences that would turn them off. Whatever the moti-vation, they wanted to teach mathematics well. Achievement in mathematics was just one of many aspects of teaching for these students. For most it was not the focus.

The university students shared another value with practicing teachers: belief in the power of experience. They put stock in what they learned from practice. They taught in the classroom, observed others teaching in the classroom, and discussed what they had seen in the classroom. This type of learning was *real*. Unless their university courses substantiated the knowledge the students gained from teaching, they discounted the courses. Karen and I tried to address this issue but it was tricky. It had to be done in a way that respected the value of experience but perhaps changed the students' perspective on or analysis of experience. For example, the university students were fond of evaluating a lesson by stating that "it went well, the kids had fun." University faculty would acknowledge that, yes, fun is good, but can we demonstrate that the elementary students also learned something from the lesson?

Another source of contention was the infamous "lesson plan." Students knew that "real" teachers didn't use elaborate lesson plans. Some cooperating teachers explicitly told the undergraduates that they never wrote a lesson plan after college. Jen, a student whose father was a principal, told me that her cooperating teacher told her to forget about lesson plans—they were just a university hoop to jump through. The university faculty had to acknowledge that classroom teachers never have the kind of time that's needed to develop the elaborate plans that are expected in university courses. So we had students observe their teachers to see if they could identify an opening/introduction to a lesson. How did the body of the lesson progress? How was it assessed? Students saw that even if teachers didn't write out lesson plans, they still used the structure and most of the elements of a lesson plan. We had to convince students that the more they consciously used lesson planning as novices, the better their lessons would be. Real teachers did use lesson plans, just not ones that were as formal.

Although the students shared important values with their teachers, one issue set them clearly apart: Students cared about their grades. They expected to receive good grades and felt betrayed if they didn't. They all felt that they were doing an inordinate amount of work, and in some semesters, they were. They would challenge grades and argue over points to a much greater extent than students in the regular education program did. Students weren't satisfied with an A—it had to be a high A. At times the value they placed on grades conflicted with another value: experience. One student heard a rumor from a friend who knew a person who had talked to a principal. The report was that principals don't like to hire applicants with too many A's on their transcripts. These people, according to the story, are likely to be perfectionists who won't do well in a school. This took on the aura of an urban myth. It was partly dispelled when the Lincoln and Forest principals said, "hogwash." Both principals told the students that they did care about academic achievement. They left out the part that the only grade they really cared about was the one from student teaching.

What did our students' experiences lead to? We hoped that they would lead to better teachers, but we couldn't be sure they would. The MIE students were more confident than most graduating pre-service teachers. But is that a sufficient goal in itself? Did we accelerate them or change them? Inservice teachers commented that the MIE students were more like third- or fourth-year veterans. Acceleration wasn't our primary goal. We wanted to change how new teachers taught and not just help them become more comfortable with the status quo. Since none of the MSU faculty involved supervised student teaching, it's difficult to judge if the MIE students taught differently from students in the regular program. As in most projects, there was no grant money for follow-up evaluation so we won't know what the long-range effects may be.

4

Inspiration and Resistance

While the purpose of MIE was to create a model collaboration between Lincoln and Forest schools and MSU, the university drove the development, implementation, and administration of the project. A university is, in some ways, the logical institution to do these jobs. It has some autonomy, expertise, and an eagerness to secure funding for projects like MIE. It also has an interest in improving teacher preparation. But because the university and the schools have different sets of values, there are also problems with locating so much of the administration at the university. At times, the university's values might conflict with what the schools want or need.

This chapter describes these values, the university's roles in the project, and the people who navigated among the project goals, university values, and school cultures.

People and Roles

MSU had responsibility for most of the development and implementation of the MIE project. Many different elements required attention, from the profound to the mundane. But even the mundane can derail the noblest intentions.

Political

Amy, the department chair of curriculum and instruction, had the lead from the start. She made the initial connections with the foundation, who funded our project. She gathered the critical people from the university. She chose the partner schools. Her role, especially given her position as department chair, was political and organizational. This was a particularly important function at the beginning of the process. Amy had authority and an understanding of the institutional issues necessary to get the project rolling. She also had to make some of the most difficult decisions.

When a preservice teacher was chronically late, was repeatedly inappropriate in the classroom, and was ejected from the classroom by his cooperating teacher, Amy was the one to deal with it.

Development

During initial conversations with the foundation, MIE was a vague idea that had to be fleshed out. This task fell to Karen. Initially she felt overwhelmed. While learning and teaching mathematics was her professional passion, she had little experience in designing a new program. She and I worried over where to even start.

Implementation

Most of the heavy lifting involved in implementing the project was also left to Karen. After developing the project, it was logical that she be in charge of implementation. Who could better understand the project's intent or details? Karen taught the undergraduates. She was the university connection to Forest and Lincoln. She led professional development activities like courses and workshops. Her role was the most demanding of all the project leaders' roles.

Evaluation

Evaluation is treated in Chapter 5, but it is important to note here that evaluation was seen by both the schools and university from the beginning as akin to research. As such, it was housed in the university. Few in the school district knew enough or cared enough to be interested in the development of the evaluation or even in the results. Evaluation is usually housed in the university in university–school collaborations. In many projects it would be advisable to hire an outside group to perform evaluation to avoid a possible conflict of interest.

Details, Details

One role that was critical to the project and yet underrecognized was administrative support. Amy's secretary, Arlene, was the keeper of the MIE budget as well as the guardian of Amy's time. She arranged all of the project details, such as travel. That was in no way a small task: One of our trips involved travel for three faculty members, eight teachers, one principal, and twenty-one undergraduates.

Although the person who provides administrative support for a project like MIE isn't usually a policy maker, she can be. Arlene was strong and capable and she was loyal to Amy. While all of these attributes are positive, they also presented some challenges. For example, Arlene would require that Karen get approval from Amy before buying anything, even a book. This annoyed Karen, who felt she had all of the responsibility but none of the authority she needed. At the same time, Amy, who was unaware that Karen had no choice, was annoyed that Karen kept asking her about trivial things. In hindsight, Arlene should have been more involved in meetings and we should have been more explicit about our expectations for her responsibilities. She saw herself as Amy's secretary, not the project secretary.

Other Faculty

At least six other faculty members taught cohort courses. Whether they recognized it or not, these courses were of three different kinds:

> courses for licensure
> courses for LiC
> courses for MIE

Each had a slightly different spin. The courses for licensure carried the stock requirements for meeting licensing requirements. The LiC layer carried additional purposes: reflective practice, university–school collaboration, and learning in a cohort. MIE added a layer of mathematics education. Participating faculty were expected to tailor their education courses to all these different purposes.

University–School Liaison

Many university–school collaborations require an intermediary. This person needs to have access to and understand both worlds. She should be "bicultural" and be able to translate between school and university personnel: "This is what the teacher meant." "Here's what 'salary savings' means." In some collaborations this job goes to a teacher with experience at the university, or to a graduate student who's familiar with the schools. In this case it went to me. I was an elementary school teacher, but I had worked at the university and I was a doctoral student in education. My role included making logistical arrangements, developing workshops, organizing miniconferences, communicating with the principals and teachers, recruiting teachers, and teaching a course to the cohort. I became a half-time employee of the university and remained half-time as a teacher, although my teaching duties dwindled. When I was asked to develop a liaison job description, it was a two-page list.

This role was tricky. I had to represent both groups without being seen as having allegiance with either. In particular, the teachers tended to be suspicious of a university representative. I had to constantly and consciously reinforce the idea that I had the interests of the teachers and schools at heart. I did, but I had to consider the intent and goals of the project as well. I had an obligation to both and sometimes their interests clashed. Using the project budget to order items that had at best a tangential connection to MIE was one of those clashes. Placing students with teachers who didn't model standards-based teaching and approving funding for a study group that didn't study placed me in a difficult position. Was I a team player and a member of the staff or was I a university person?

Sometimes, the pressure came from the university. Once Karen and I struggled over whether to drop a student from the program. He was chronically unprepared for the lessons he was scheduled to teach. Several times he failed to even show up. I met with him and his supervising teacher, a highly structured yet supportive soul, and we developed a contract. But he continued to be a problem. In a private meeting with Amy, I asked that he be removed from the program. She was reluctant and suggested that we assign him to another class with a different teacher. I felt pressure to agree but held my ground. I knew that it would be disrespectful of the teacher to find this student a different placement. In the end, Amy conceded and the student was asked to leave. His teacher thanked me and she remained a supportive force for the project in the school.

This liaison position was most critical in the first half of the project when the university and school first started to interact. At that point people were just developing their ideas about the project and each other. It became a more mundane job when things started going smoothly. Relationships between Karen and many of the teachers developed their own momentum. As trust grew, the challenge of my job diminished.

Cohort Mentor

The cohort was supposed to get a university faculty member as a mentor/leader. As discussed in other chapters, this person would guide the group, monitor the dynamics, visit their classrooms, and help the students reflect on their experiences. This task should logically have gone to Karen. In the first year, MSU didn't assign anyone. In the second year, a faculty member who had no investment in the project assumed the responsibility. In the third year, the action research professor took over. She met with the students but never came to the schools. In three years, there was no consistent faculty presence in the cohort social structure.

Issues

Amy was a master at political issues. She was also more than willing to relinquish authority. She didn't second-guess or micromanage. Karen was also well-suited to her role. She had a passion for mathematics teaching and learning. Her immense respect for teachers helped her to build their trust. Arlene was an extremely competent secretary. She knew the university and she knew Amy. I was well positioned for my role as well. I was a teacher at the school and also familiar with the university.

But with 20/20 hindsight, I see some things we should have done differently. The most prominent problem we had was the location of authority. Karen and I had been responsible for the project but lacked authority. I had to organize workshops and Karen had to teach them, but I couldn't access the school budget and Karen couldn't order a book without Amy's permission. The people who develop and implement any project should have access to the budget and anything else that affects implementation.

Just as the lines of budget authority should have been more explicit, so should the rules for participation have been. Faculty became involved because they had taught past courses for LiC, not because of any commitment to the MIE project. The project gave them equipment, such as new computers, and paid for time to work mathematics into their curricula. But they weren't recruited because of interest, they were grafted onto the project. As a result, they kept doing what they always had—teaching their courses. They didn't become involved in Lincoln and Forest or in changing their curricula. Karen, as an untenured faculty member, had no authority to make them. We should have made the rules for participation more explicit: To get a new computer, we expect this, for instance. No one intentionally misled anyone.

While my university side worked well, there was potential for problems that should have been anticipated. I was a graduate student working on my dissertation, and could have been pressured to accommodate the university. I wasn't. But if I were to give advice to those implementing a similar project, I would caution them to give the liaison as much authority as any faculty member or school authority had. Many of the faculty members who were involved in the MIE project were on my Ph.D. committee. It was never a conflict, but it could have been.

Work with the Schools

One of the project leaders' most basic assumptions was that faculty would become more involved with the schools and the borders between MSU and Lincoln-Forest would be blurred. We expected university involvement in schools to have a powerful impact. Faculty members' work would be more sophisticated if they better understood school life. Their research would have more impact on practice and the preparation of new teachers would benefit if faculty were familiar with school work. These assumptions might seem obvious, but they proved the most difficult part of the project to implement.

In the Classroom

We intended that the university's role in the project would extend beyond placing students with mentor teachers. University faculty would be active in teaching, assisting, and observing in the classroom. This would have several benefits:

- It would provide some in-classroom time for professors. It would make sense for professors who prepare new teachers to have experience in the classroom, but they often don't, especially at research universities.

- It could provide a shared experience for the school staff and MSU faculty members, which could lead to conversations that created a bridge between the university and the schools.
- The university preservice teachers would see university and schools as working toward the same goals.
- It would give faculty members ideas for research that they could do either together with the classroom teacher or alone.

Things didn't work out exactly as planned. Of the seven faculty members who were involved with the undergraduates, only Karen showed up in the classroom to teach. But Karen's role was always to model instruction. She came as the expert willing to share trade secrets, and she never observed other teachers or debriefed a lesson. Karen's visits became, unfortunately, a project public relations tool: be seen in the classroom, model a new technique, and give the teacher a break from the classroom. This was important, but it didn't approach the full range of "shared experience" we had hoped for.

In Research

Project leaders also made the assumption that reflective practice in the schools could be married to research in the university. A faculty member could study a classroom in order to better understand teaching, and the teacher could collect and use the same data to improve or change some aspect of her practice. Because Karen was the only faculty member with any presence in the schools, she was the only one to conduct classroom research. With one fifth-grade teacher she developed an NCTM presentation on fractions. It wasn't exactly research, but it was "scholarly." They searched the literature on learning fractions, developed some lessons together, then experimented with the lessons by teaching them. The teacher benefited from systematically looking at student understanding and Karen benefited by researching conceptual development of fractions. The only other attempt for a teacher-faculty study group (discussed in Chapter 2) failed because the participants didn't share the same interests. The teachers agreed to participate through loyalty to Karen and the faculty agreed because of access to research funding. There wasn't enough of a sense common purpose to maintain interest.

There was one other person doing research—me. I needed to collect data for my dissertation. The only way to do it while working full time was to use the project. That was a luxury in some ways. I was able to multitask, making my work for MIE count twice. But it also presented difficulties—I was too close to the project to give truly independent opinions. I also began investing even more time into the project. I lived and breathed MIE. This led to some possibilities for conflict. Could I say anything negative about MIE in my dissertation? Fortunately, Amy and Karen didn't expect me to mince words. I know that Amy thought I was too negative in some of my assessments, but she never expected me to change anything. Karen may have thought I was too generous in some of my conclusions, but she too wouldn't have expected me to alter any part of my dissertation. My dissertation work also put me in a precarious position at school. Did I dare to say anything critical? Would teachers and principals be honest with me about MIE if they knew I was analyzing the project for my dissertation? Fortunately, the difficulty never arose.

Distance

The faculty members' activities presented some difficulties. Several of those problems have already been discussed in other chapters, but there are two issues particularly worthy of note.

It seems obvious, but the issues of time and distance are important. Forest and Lincoln are forty-some miles away from MSU, which discouraged all but the most dedicated faculty members from becoming involved at the schools. Faculty taught, at most, one class for the cohort in a semester. It wasn't realistic to expect them to drive for two hours to make a school visit. They had other courses and responsibilities. They taught courses, did their research and writing, and served on committees. If the schools had been closer or if they had had more motivation or a sense of purpose about participating, faculty members might have played a larger role in the schools.

Work with Preservice Students

Our initial project proposal outlined several changes to the preservice program. One was that the seven professors involved would "use mathematics as a unifying theme across their courses."

Karen and I envisioned mathematics being incorporated into the foundations course and the course in multicultural education. The foundations course could include mathematics references in discussions of equity. The curriculum shifts of the past century could be illustrated with examples of mathematics curricula. We purchased an elementary mathematics curriculum series that taught mathematics through social issues and gave it to the foundations professor. We also thought that there were plenty of connections for using math in the multicultural class. But then we ran into something called "academic freedom." Faculty expected professional autonomy. They taught their own classes with materials and syllabi that they designed to meet their own standards.

Karen took the lead in discussing the connection to mathematics with the professors who would teach these courses. One professor, Richard, had poured his soul into the development of LiC. As we began writing the MIE proposal I reread the original proposal for the design of the LiC program. It was grand and elegant. It envisioned substantial participation from both university faculty and school faculty. Preservice students would blend research and practice to become teachers of a new type. LiC would create "simultaneous renewal." But the program's evolution through bureaucratic expedience left Richard feeling betrayed. LiC got sliced and diced into something very different from the original plan. Involvement from school faculty was gone. No teachers or school administrators attended the steering meetings. Why? They were held during school hours. Why not change the hours? It wouldn't be convenient for university members. The proposed democracy and education class? Gone. Why? Because it was co-taught between faculty in two departments, it was difficult to negotiate within the university's system of faculty load. And neither department developed an investment in the class. Eventually nothing was left of Richard's original design aside from a student cohort and extended field experiences. So Richard was bitter. But he liked Karen. He admired her for being honest and ethical. Karen had some conversations with him about MIE and his course. They discussed the notion that the MIE LiC cohort would be mathematics focused. Grant money was available to support faculty work as they tweaked courses to have a math flavor. Karen also talked with Andie, who taught the foundations course. On the surface, Andie and Richard appeared interested. Karen and I were encouraged. But attempts to inject a connection to math in their courses never happened. Until the third semester, there was nothing in the coursework or field experiences that distinguished the MIE group from the other LiC cohorts. They wouldn't get mathematics as part of any education course they took before the mathematics methods course at the end of their junior year. What happened? Poor communication? Possibly. We didn't receive notice about our proposal being accepted until the start of the school year and there wasn't much time to organize. What we thought were agreements may have seemed like preliminary conversations to others.

Now that I have been in an MSU faculty position for a year, I can see other problems with the way Karen and I approached faculty members. First, Andie and Richard had no investment in MIE because they weren't part of the planning. We described what we wanted their participation to be without getting their input, so we were asking them for a favor rather than integrating them into the project. Second, they had well-developed courses that had evolved from careful thought and deliberation about what preservice teachers need to know. There is an integrity and structure to such courses that is not easily changed. The idea of "tweaking" them to incorporate mathematics is harder than it sounds.

Values

The university culture has a set of values, many of which differ significantly from the values held in the schools.

Research

MSU faculty members valued research. MIE provided opportunities to conduct research and produce publications. Karen wrote guidelines for the faculty to develop and conduct small research projects with MIE funds. This seed money was intended to develop faculty interest in participation. Unfortunately, it apparently wasn't enough to entice faculty members into the schools.

Evaluation

Evaluation was an important consideration for the university side. The foundation expected a detailed evaluation. This project was its largest national grant award, so it expected substantial accountability. The university hired a research institute to help construct and conduct the evaluation. The schools saw this as part of the university research function and didn't want to contribute funds toward the evaluation. An evaluation committee was formed that included school staff, but they gradually stopped attending meetings. Indeed, in some ways the school district tried to protect the schools from evaluation by the university. The district evaluation and assessment office insisted on reviewing all evaluation instruments used in the schools and required many changes before approving several of the surveys and other tools.

Student Placements

The university was interested in getting appropriate placements for the preservice students. Since the students spent a significant amount of time in the schools, the placements were considered to be especially important. One faculty member and several teachers spent a lot of time matching students with appropriate teachers. Students with weak organizational skills were placed with teachers who could model those skills. A student with an off-beat personality was placed with teachers who were less traditional or judgmental. This level of consideration in placements wouldn't have been possible in MSU's regular teacher preparation program.

Knowledge of Content and Pedagogy

Methods faculty members believed that preservice teachers needed a certain level of knowledge. They felt that their professional integrity would be compromised if the preservice students in MIE didn't receive the same level of subject coverage as students in the regular program. They believed that their task was to make sure that the students got the same, if not more, information than they would have in the regular program. Anything less would be "unethical" or "professional malpractice." Providing this level of information proved difficult because the time students spent in the field was taken out of the time they had in class. During the methods semester, students lost six weeks of university class time. In the earlier years of LiC, it was assumed that the participants elementary teachers would teach what the students missed in class. This was naive, according to faculty members who had been involved from the beginning: In reality, some content the university faculty valued wasn't necessarily taught in the schools at all.

Grading

The university methods faculty believed, as did the undergraduate students, that grading should be fair. Their standards were different from the students', however. The students thought they should be evaluated on field experience, but the university faculty were concerned that would inflate the grades compared to those of students in regular methods classes. The attempts at integrating mathematics into other courses helped to inflate grades because faculty members gave students the benefit of the doubt: If an instructor graded a paper outside her own content area, she tended to be lenient. Faculty members also had a difficult time evaluating assignments that were not of their own design.

Faculty Control

The university faculty believed that they deserved and should command control over the curriculum and classroom decisions. They were concerned that the students were trying to assume that control. They thought the students were critical and demanding of them. Students constantly tried to negotiate assignments. In a faculty focus group conversation about student input on curricular decisions, one methods instructor suggested that faculty should be in control of such decisions. She started to temper her remarks by saying that she might not be smarter than the students. Another instructor stopped her: "You are smarter than they are. You have a depth and breadth of knowledge that you have had the opportunity to develop." The faculty valued the empowerment of the students, but as one MIE student put it, "You told us we would become empowered but when we were, you didn't know what to do with it."

Community

Faculty members wanted the students to develop a sense of community in their classes and at the schools, but they worried that those were mutually exclusive. It was difficult for faculty to be part of the school communities. The students noticed their absence and didn't understand it. In focus groups and interviews, teachers reported that they enjoyed seeing faculty in the halls and wished that they could be in the schools more.

Funding and Professional Organizations

The MIE project received a substantial subsidy from its corporate partner. External funding for such projects is a priority because it extends a university's resources. If part of Karen's salary is paid by a grant, for example, the university can use that money to hire others. Part of the university interest in the foundation was in the financial resources it offered. But the interest also came from respect. The faculty members knew and respected the opinions of foundation representatives. As the project leaders proposed new activities or organized grant extensions we tried to be consistent with what the foundation valued.

The Schools

The MIE faculty members were consistently sensitive to what teachers and principals wanted and needed. Teacher feedback was highly valued by faculty. My position as a school-based representative often involved relaying messages from the schools to the university or serving as an advocate or translator for the schools. The schools' needs and desires were so respected by the project leaders that they were sometimes accommodated even against the MIE faculty members' better judgment, particularly in the area of student teacher placement.

The grant application was submitted to the foundation as a joint project between the schools and the university and the money was awarded to both. There was no institutional way to share responsibility. The money had to go to one and then be shared with the other. It was in the interests of the faculty for the grant money to come through the university. The university became the primary institution responsible for budget, reports, and evaluation, and the schools in effect became subcontractors.

Promotion and Tenure

Faculty members had to attend to other institutional values as well. Karen, the workhorse for this project, was an untenured assistant faculty member at the beginning of the MIE project. The grant award provided her with both advantages and challenges within the university. It was to her advantage to be one of the principal investigators, but to her disadvantage that the project required an inordinate amount of time in the schools that detracted from the time she needed to write and conduct research. The distance to the schools and the number of meetings at the school sites put her in a difficult situation. Her work in classrooms and doing workshops fell into the category of "service." Service at a land-grant university should weigh heavily in favor of promotion and tenure, but, unfortunately, it doesn't. The amount of time that Karen spent at the schools was much less valued by her tenure committee than her publication record was. Karen did get tenure, but the process would have been easier if she had had more time to write and publish.

The university's contribution to the project was critical. It was a blend of inspiration, control, and resistance. The inspiration for and development of the project were almost totally in the hands of the university: MIE was the university's baby. Amy, who enlisted Karen, located the funding and found the school partners. The university had budget accountability and control of most of the inservice professional development as well as preservice education.

While the university provided much of the inspiration and perspiration, it also put up resistance to the project, largely as a result of the institutional culture. The system of tenure and promotion posed obstacles for Karen's participation in the schools. Faculty members' focus on content worked against their incorporating mathematics into their courses. The university didn't value student teaching enough to send regular faculty members to supervise, leaving this most critical aspect of a teacher's development in the hands of people who weren't involved with the students' university education.

The people at the university all had good intentions. The goals of the university efforts were noble: to improve teacher preparation and to extend university involvement with the schools. The institutional organization forced those goals to fit existing university structures and values. This had the consequence, however unintentional, of undermining the MIE goals.

5

The Demonstration
of Achievements

Few people who dream of a new project place evaluation at the forefront. The MIE project leaders were no exception. We wanted to think about the different opportunities that the project would make available to teachers. We imagined lively classrooms where mathematics lived and breathed. We saw teachers studying and struggling over lessons and assessment. The one thing we didn't put any thought into in planning the project was how a good evaluation plan could help us achieve our goals.

I'm not sure why evaluation was such an afterthought. It's not that we were trying to avoid accountability; we simply didn't know much about evaluation or realize the potential of a good plan focusing on formative evaluation. We were naive about the power that lies behind committing to outcomes. If we spend this money, exactly what will the affected classrooms look like? How will we know whether we are successful or not? It's similar to ongoing assessment in the classroom: How can we tell if a lesson meets the teacher's goals? When I teach preservice teachers in their first methods courses, they often struggle over assessment, but I hammer them with how important it is to know if a lesson was successful. The same accountability should be expected of those of us who try to change teaching—especially when we're doing it with someone else's money. How will we know we've met our objectives? How can we gauge our work and make improvements and adjustments as we go along? And how can we communicate our learning to others to help improve other projects?

Stakeholders

Evaluation efforts must be strong in order to describe, justify, and improve what a project does. The audience for this information is expanding. In any large project there are many stakeholders, the people and organizations that have an investment in the project's outcome. Some will have an investment in the success of a new project; others may have an investment in maintaining the status quo. Some will be wildly enthusiastic about the project and others will be suspicious, ambivalent, or hostile.

The first groups of stakeholders that the MIE project leaders worked with were those at the university. This was not a single homogeneous entity. There were different groups with different agendas. The most deeply invested stakeholders at the university were the faculty, many of whom were involved. Amy's interest was technical. As project director she needed to make certain that the obligations to the foundation and to the university were fulfilled. She was also interested in promoting Karen's research. As department chair, Amy was responsible for faculty development. Untenured professors need to develop outside funding and generate research and writing opportunities. This project grant provided such resources. Karen had never been involved with a project of this scale. She wanted Amy's guidance and felt that Amy should make the final decisions and guide the evaluation. Karen intended to lend her own strengths in teaching and researching student learning, but believed that project evaluation was outside her realm of interests and expertise.

Several professors taught courses in the project but none were involved in evaluation until the students' mega-methods semester, which comes past the halfway point in the program. The mega-methods faculty varied in our interest in the evaluation. Karen and I were invested in getting good data, but at least one of the other mega-methods faculty said point-blank that she cared only about teaching undergraduates how to teach reading, she couldn't have cared less about the MIE project. A couple of faculty members tried to do some research with teachers, but none of them cared about the project evaluation. They had bit parts, and the overall success of the project was of little, if any, interest to them. They took no part in the evaluation.

The undergraduate preservice teachers also had a stake in the project. A lot was demanded of them. They had extra course requirements, more commuting time, and more time in the field than students in the regular program. They attended more meetings and traveled together. While these represented opportunities, they also demanded a big time investment. Would the investment pay off for them as future teachers? Would they be better prepared to teach mathematics? Would they be more comfortable and effective in the classroom? If not, what was the point? But despite these concerns, they gave little thought to the evaluation. In fact, they were at times hostile to it. Evaluation was just one more drain on their time and they didn't welcome it. Although the students met with evaluators only a few times a year, many would groan and roll their eyes at the mention of another survey or interview. I don't remember if we explained the value of evaluation to the preservice teachers, but if we did, we made a poor job of it.

There was one more major university stakeholder in the MIE project: the administrator of the LiC program. LiC in general was expensive, with costs including a lot of faculty involvement, small classes, and travel for the students. There had to be a documented advantage in order to justify LiC. While in some ways LiC was a darling of the college of education, some faculty resented it because of the resources it drained. Others felt it was a trophy without substance—a PR opportunity. Some modest evaluation of LiC had revealed that its graduates were happy and its students dropped out at a slightly lower rate. But the program needed more to justify it. Despite this, the LiC administrator had no involvement in the MIE project evaluation. Although it's obvious to me now, it never occurred to me during the life of the project that the LiC administrator should have been included in organizing data collection for MIE. She could have offered a lot. She might have helped us to develop our questions in a more sophisticated way. But we didn't talk to her. There was some sense of competition. We were the *math* cohort. We were special. I imagine that the administrator might have resented us—after all, we hijacked her program with a pot of money.

The school district administrators were another important group of stakeholders. They were ultimately responsible for student achievement and the appropriate use of district resources. They also felt that they needed to protect their teachers and staff members from additional drains on their time and energy. So even though this project promised the schools a significant amount of money, the district administrators weren't going to jump at this opportunity without careful scrutiny. They asked the project leaders to present our proposal at an administrators' meeting. Their questions were focused but not harsh. What did we expect to accomplish? How did we expect the project to affect teachers, students, and school communities? What impact would it have on teacher time? School resources? The administrators needed to be comfortable with the focus and the logistics of the grant.

The school district's testing and evaluation office protected the district's interests. The biggest challenge in getting district approval for the project was to satisfy the district evaluation team. We sent a copy of the proposal to the two chief district evaluation experts and scheduled a meeting with them at Lincoln. They arrived looking very serious. Their tattered copies of the proposal were decorated with Post-it notes and highlighting pens. The margins contained more text than the original proposal. They asked questions about everything. Although some of their questions were comically trivial, others were not. Their goal, which they stated often, was to protect the children and teachers from university research. They didn't want children and teachers to be guinea pigs just to advance someone's university career. They eventually agreed to support the project, but they made it clear that they wanted approval of any evaluation effort that involved children, teachers, parents, or district staff, which ultimately gave them veto power over half of the evaluation.

Other stakeholders had considerable interest in the outcome of the project but had little input or interest in its evaluation. Parents and other community members wanted to know how well their children were doing and that school resources were being used well. They wanted the best teachers and resources for their kids and to know what was happening in the classroom. Despite the fact that the parents had the biggest stake in the outcome— their children's education—their involvement and contribution to the evaluation and to the project were negligible. We initially tried to include a Lincoln parent in the planning, but he expressed uncertainty about what role he should assume. Truthfully, we didn't know either. We included him only because we knew we should have parent input, but we were clueless about what he should contribute. He eventually stopped coming to meetings, and no one replaced him. The parent component of the evaluation was reduced to attendance records and a small survey from Family Math Nights at Lincoln.

After parents, teachers had the second greatest stake. The project had designs on their time and energy. We wanted to change the way they taught mathematics. More demands were made on them than on anyone else, except perhaps the preservice teachers.

They treated most of the evaluation efforts as an annoyance. When the time came to do the initial survey, the teachers seemed to resent it because it took more time away from their teaching. They didn't seem to appreciate the value of the evaluation or their role in it. We never asked the teachers what they wanted to find out so that the evaluation could give them information they needed to teach better. In hindsight, that would have been a logical step. There was a larger obstacle to teacher participation in evaluation: Some of the teachers didn't value research. Although there are distinctions between evaluation and research, these teachers saw them as one and the same.

The funder of a project will also want to know how the project worked and how it might inform other projects. Our contacts at the foundation were accountable to a corporate hierarchy. They had to justify their choices as well as or better than we did. They wanted evaluation that would give them solid evidence of the project's value and that would help them to improve and refine their expectations of new projects.

Who Does the Evaluation?

Traditionally, evaluators come from outside a project because outsiders are more likely to be objective. If someone from inside the project does an evaluation, it is suspect. The evaluation would be assumed to have a built-in bias because of personal investment. Perhaps they would see only the positive parts, or exaggerate the positive in order to receive more funding. But there are positive aspects of using internal evaluators, too. People who work with a project on a daily basis have insights that others don't. They really want to know what works and what doesn't. Formative assessment is very important to them.

We chose evaluators who were associated with the college of education at MSU. The evaluation group was an independent center within the college, although the director was a college faculty member. The group provided evaluation services for districts and projects across the state as well as serving as the lead evaluator for virtually all of the grants run through the college. These folks assumed charge of the MIE project evaluation efforts. Their stake in the project stemmed from their responsibility for the contract. Whether we failed or succeeded did not concern them.

There were a host of graduate students assigned to project evaluation at different points. One was a fellow student and personal friend of mine. I was nervous about having her pass judgment on my work. My skin was getting thicker, but it still wasn't tough enough to handle the judgment of my peers.

There was a tendency by Karen and myself to see evaluation as a necessary evil—with the emphasis on evil. It didn't help that we were dealing with outside evaluators. How could they possibly understand our project? We didn't see the evaluators as critical friends, but as detectives inquiring into our personal lives. We wanted to look good, so we emphasized the positive in talking with them about the project.

In hindsight it's obvious that the evaluation could have profited from broader participation. If all of those with stakes in the outcome of MIE had provided guidance in the evaluation plan, the plan would have been stronger. It might also have been greeted with more enthusiasm than it was.

From Needs to Purpose and Proposal

The most logical first step of an evaluation is to establish a need. Fortunately for us, that proved to be quite easy. There has been considerable focus on the sorry state of mathematics understanding among students and elementary school teachers. The references were easy to locate. We also had the advantage of a recent statewide survey that had been conducted by our evaluation group. It verified that teachers in the state had little knowledge of the national standards for teaching math. More than 60 percent had no knowledge of the standards for their own grade level. Even fewer knew anything about standards for other grades. It also helped that the foundation was already invested in the work. The project leaders' job became to prove that we knew the literature. Our proposal documented the challenges in teaching mathematics in ways that are consistent with the standards: Texts are sometimes incompatible with reform standards; assessments often do not reflect the types of understanding emphasized in standards; teachers haven't had the opportunity to talk with other teachers about teaching—especially teaching in ways that they have never experienced personally.

But what would the project's goal be? If we had to distill it to a bumper-sticker slogan, what would it say? Our goal, as stated in the executive summary of our proposal, was to "create a mathematically rich environment where K–12 students, K–12 teachers, preservice teachers, teacher education faculty, parents, and community learn, collaborate, and model the best practices in mathematics education." Here is where some friendly feedback from an evaluator would have been helpful. Just what would a "mathematically rich environment" look like? How would we know when we'd achieved it?

The more challenging task was to develop strategies to meet our goal. How could we improve student understanding and appreciation of mathematics through preservice and inservice education? The proposal was broken down into three categories: preservice education, inservice education, and MSU faculty development. Within each category we planned to make changes in curriculum, teaching, learning, and research.

According to our proposal, the curriculum of the MSU preservice students would expose them to "intensive field-based learning, a cohort with which to identify, and learning experiences with an emphasis on integration." Mathematics was to be the unifying theme. Additional mathematics courses were suggested, as well as the infusion of mathematics in all of the coursework. The students would demonstrate their new understandings through a portfolio that would be constructed with the help of an MSU faculty member.

The MSU students were to spend an average of about one-third of their six project semesters in the schools. At Forest and Lincoln they were expected to complete a variety of relevant field-based tasks to further their understanding of the teaching profession, with a particular emphasis on the teaching of all subjects in the context of mathematics.

The students would conduct an action research project in a Lincoln or Forest classroom as coursework. They would consider a problem or question encountered during their learning experiences, study it, analyze it, and make a suggestion for improving practice. This research project would encourage students to become more reflective in their teaching and to strive to continually learn and grow as educators.

The educators at Lincoln and Forest would engage in a set of parallel activities to improve mathematics learning. A series of workshops and graduate-level MSU courses would address student and community needs, curriculum design, use of instructional technology, assessment, and instructional strategies. The existing district curriculum, which had recently changed to a standards-based program, would be tilted toward a connection to other content areas and real-world applications of mathematics. The Lincoln-Forest teachers would be encouraged to travel, funded by MIE, to NCTM regional and national conferences. In addition to their regular classroom duties, the teachers would assume responsibility for the education of MSU preservice teachers. The MSU students would learn at the elbows of the inservice teachers. The MSU student, inservice teacher, and MSU faculty member involved in supervision would become a team invested in extending their understanding of teaching and learning. All three would participate in research, either action research or research intended for a wider audience.

The MSU faculty would integrate mathematics into their assignments and teaching. In their introduction to teaching methods courses, students would study NCTM journals such as *Teaching Children Mathematics* or *Mathematics Teaching in Middle School* instead of generic materials. The MSU faculty would teach together with Lincoln-Forest teachers to apply models of integration and cooperative teaching. In addition, the MSU faculty, who were unidentified in the proposal, would teach for Lincoln-Forest teachers so they would have more time to attend to their own professional and curriculum development. It was hoped that through teaching in the schools, the MSU faculty would learn more about the development and changing academic needs of elementary school students.

MIE work would also provide fodder for faculty members' educational research. Nine major research projects were listed as possibilities. They ran from the very broad (studying changes in the mathematics teaching of inservice or preservice teachers) to the very specific (the effects of extended field experiences at one site). Faculty might work with inservice teachers or on their own to extend the project's understanding of professional learning or students' understanding of mathematics.

The proposal named the Lincoln-Forest community as partners. Community members were invited to planning meetings. Even though they stopped coming, they were still welcome. Meetings were planned for parent and community education. Lunch-bag Learning was a series sponsored by Lincoln to inform parents about curriculum and events. Parents were provided with a school lunch and participated in activities and discussion about the school curriculum as they munched on tater tots. Family Math Nights were also planned to include and inform parents about their children's education.

Timing

The project leaders established contact with the evaluators early, before the proposal was submitted. Even so, it was a little late. The evaluation plan was developed after the grant proposal had its basic design. We could have had a more solid proposal if we had worked with the evaluators from the very beginning. The formative assessment should have started with our initial brainstorming. What would these classrooms look like, exactly? How could we tell if we met our goals? How would the MIE undergraduates be different from their peers in the regular program?

Evaluation Questions

This project was multifaceted. Evaluation had to be equally multifaceted. The questions had to be deep and informative. What did we hope to find out? We had developed our list of proposed activities first, largely without input from our evaluators. Now we needed to work with the evaluators to develop questions to guide our data collection.

Accountability

This was the easiest to develop. It is a first step that seems obvious but still has to happen. Did we do what we said we would do? Did we offer workshops and classes? Did teachers participate? Were Family Math Nights held? Did people come? Did faculty teach at the elementary schools? These were questions whose answers were simple.

Effectiveness

Effectiveness is really a measure of participant satisfaction. Did those who participated in MIE activities like them? Did they see a value to them? Our questions here were deeper than the data we collected. For example, the question "Were Family Math Nights a good way to involve parents in their child's education?" was answered through a brief satisfaction survey we asked parents to fill out. Whether or not these nights were a good way to involve parents is much more complicated. In many evaluations of programs, such as those funded by Eisenhower grants, evaluation goes no further than this. Did you do what you said, and did they like it? With an increasing emphasis on impact, evidence of participant satisfaction is no longer sufficient.

We must also answer the question "What difference did it make?" Did classroom teaching change in a way we hoped? Did teachers pay more attention to children's mathematical reasoning? Did parents better understand the goals of their children's mathematics program? Could the parents help their children more at home? After three years of intensive work, did the graduating MSU students teach in a way that was different from students who went through the regular program. These questions, along with others, formed the core of what we needed to know about effectiveness.

Impact

Questions about the project's impact address the heart of what we hoped to do. How were teachers, students, and faculty different as a result of our efforts? Did attitudes toward mathematics change? We even dared to ask if achievement improved for Lincoln-Forest students. The first two categories are important: Obviously, we should do what we said we'd do and do it well enough that folks appreciate it. But our actions are meaningless unless they have an impact—changing attitudes and learning.

Organization

The changes we hoped for would take place in an organizational context. We knew that the institutions—both the schools and the university—would have to accommodate the activities. They could work in numerous ways to support or undermine the project. We tried to document the ways in which the institutions affected the activities and outcomes of the project. What supports were available? What obstacles arose? What accommodations did the institutions make to guarantee success?

Data Collection

Table 2 summarizes the data collection plan, delineating the major project activities and how they were evaluated.

TABLE 2.

	Question	Type	Source	Method	Time
Accountability	• Did participants complete courses and workshops?	Record data	Staffs	Records	End of year
	• Were Family Math Nights and brown-bag lunches held?	Record data	Schools	Records	End of year
	• Did staffs participate in exchange teaching?	Records, papers	Staffs	Records	End of year
	• Did staffs attend or present at conferences?	Record data	Staffs	Records	End of year
	• Did MSU faculty integrate math into education courses?	Record data, opinions	MSU students and faculty	Records and interviews	End of semester
Effectiveness	• Did participants find activities valuable?			Questionaire	End of workshop
	• Were Family Math Nights and brown-bag lunches good ways to involve parents in education?	Satisfaction surveys	MSU students and faculty and L-F teachers	Focus group	End of activity
	• Was exchange teaching worthwhile?			Focus group	End of exchange
	• Was collaboration effective?			Focus group	annually

(continues)

	Question	Type	Source	Method	Time
Impact	• Did L-F teachers' attitudes about mathematics change?	Survey	L-F teachers	Questionaire	Pre-post
	• Did parents' attitudes change?	Survey	L-F parents	Questionaire	Pre-post
	• Did L-F students' achievement in mathematics change?	Achievement tests	L-F students	Norm-referenced standardized test or district test	Pre-post
	• Did L-F students' attitudes about mathematics change?	Survey	L-F students	Questionaire	Pre-post
	• Did MSU students' attitudes about mathematics change?	Survey	MSU students	Questionaire	Pre-post
Organization	What organizational factors facilitated or inhibited changes?	Record data, opinions	MIE staff	Interviews	End of year
Unexpected	What changes occurred that were not expected?	Record data, opinions	MIE staff	Interviews	End of year

Our data collection tools included both quantitative and qualitative elements. The quantitative tools ranged from the most simple aspect of the evaluation (documenting attendance) to the most complex of issues (student achievement scores).

Quantitative Data

We developed surveys that asked respondents if they enjoyed the project activity and if they might implement ideas from the activity. The responses were tabulated. Unfortunately, because of the lack of communication between the project administrators and the project evaluators, many of the workshops were not evaluated. We knew who and how many had attended, but we had no inkling about their satisfaction with the activity. Did the teachers who participated in the manipulatives workshop like it? Use the ideas? No one knew.

Parental attitude was evaluated only once. A parent survey was done at the first Family Math Night. It essentially described parents' satisfaction with the event. The parents in attendance enjoyed the evening, but whether their knowledge or attitudes about their children's mathematics education changed was uncharted. The parents who attended tended to be those who appreciated teachers' efforts and the results of the survey were extremely positive. Neither parents nor the broader community were mentioned in the final evaluation report to the foundation.

At an initial joint faculty meeting of Forest and Lincoln teachers (a rare event), a survey of teacher practice and knowledge of the NCTM standards was conducted. The survey was put together using existing surveys together with a few items that were designed specifically for our project. It included questions about familiarity with the NCTM standards as well as questions about attitudes toward mathematics and teachers' ability to teach it and use it. The survey was administered again when the project ended, four years later. The university students completed a similar survey as they began their involvement. They were surveyed again when they graduated, three years after the initial survey.

Another quantitative measure we proposed to evaluate was changes in student achievement. Historically there has been little attention paid to actual changes in the classroom and in learning. But with increasing demands for accountability, many levels of stakeholders, especially at the district and policy levels, require increased documentation of improved student understanding. School districts will be much more likely to fund professional development in mathematics if they can see that it makes a difference in student achievement.

The project's emphasis on student achievement was perhaps the most slippery piece to document. There are huge numbers of variables that influence student achievement, and there are many different definitions of student achievement. Districts often define student achievement through standardized tests. Teachers usually have a broader, multifaceted perspective on student learning. Our assessments would have to capture the needs of both. We planned to compare student achievement data from before and after the project. We would also use surveys, designed for use with elementary-age children, in an effort to gauge student attitudes.

Qualitative Data

The larger volume of data came from qualitative measures. We planned to conduct interviews of individual participants from many different aspects of the project: administrators, teachers, preservice teachers, university faculty, and community members. We also planned to conduct focus groups, because group dynamics can create a rich discussion that individual interviews may miss.

Focus groups were convened twice for both the teachers and the university students. The mega-methods faculty were interviewed at the conclusion of the mega-methods semester. The focus groups were a particularly rich source of data. The interplay between the participants provided an opportunity for teachers, preservice students, and university faculty to share their experiences, successes, and challenges. This is one point at which there was an advantage to having outside evaluators. Everyone opened up to the outsiders.

Annual Reports

The foundation required a summary report from each year of the project. One of our bigger surprises was that writing the annual report became a pleasant way to sit back and reflect upon the year. It provided balance and a way to slow down and appreciate our own efforts. We got to focus on the workshops, classes, study groups, travel, and coteaching rather than on the few thorns.

Even if the foundation had not required this document, we would have found it necessary to invent it.

There is a danger in turning an annual report into a celebration of the year's accomplishments: The report can lose its value as a formative assessment tool. We never went beyond accountability in our annual reports. We listed all of the participants and all of the sponsored events, but we never included data on effectiveness or impact. That was partly intentional. Since our continued funding was partly dependent on the report, we wanted it to be positive. We might mention a few warts, but we never mentioned their size.

Missing Pieces

There were some obvious elements missing from the evaluation plan. Our goal was to affect how the mathematics classroom looks and feels—how teachers and students interact to learn mathematics. Despite the importance of this goal, there was no evaluation component that involved classroom teaching. We don't know how teachers taught before or after the project. In focus groups, we asked teachers if they attended to their mathematics teaching differently. Their answers provided us with some indications, but this type of self-reporting is unreliable. Teachers may think they do things differently when they actually don't. Or, at the opposite extreme, teachers may come to realize how complicated teaching reform is and underreport the magnitude of the changes they have implemented. In any case, some classroom observation data would have improved our evaluation. Such information is difficult to gather. Many teachers are reluctant to have outsiders come in to observe their classes. They see the potential for the observer to sit in judgment of their teaching. Such evaluation is uncomfortable, at best. But I could think of many teachers who would have been game. This is an area that I wish we had worked on—opening up the classroom and creating dialogue about teaching.

Documenting teachers' changes in practice is also important because another measure of improved teaching, student achievement, may lag behind the interventions. Student achievement is unlikely to change immediately because teachers need time to practice and assimilate new ideas. Achievement is more likely to dip as new practices are tried. If changes in student achievement and attitudes are not immediate, are there any precursors that indicate that positive changes will occur? It would have helped tremendously if we could have identified behaviors that suggested that changes were on track to result in positive student outcomes. If we could have pointed to constellations of classroom factors that predicted higher student achievement, we could have justified and improved our efforts. We could also have begged for something that districts are short of in this high-stakes environment: their patience.

Another type of information that was missing was evaluation of teachers' content knowledge. In order to teach mathematics for understanding, you have to understand mathematics. We offered several content-based graduate courses and we assumed that teachers who took them learned more content. But there may be other ways to improve teachers' understanding of content. There could be a run-off effect of content understanding from activities that concentrate on pedagogy. But we missed the opportunity to gauge this.

There are other lines of evidence that were not pursued. Table 2 identifies a number of questions for which data was needed from Lincoln-Forest students. These data-collection activities were never conducted. Students weren't interviewed or surveyed. They were tested, but an analysis of the tests wasn't included in our project reports. Students are a tricky lot to study. First, parents and the district have to give permission. The district is especially, for good reason, guarded about giving that permission. Second, how reliable are surveys of students? The responses from a kindergartner may be amusing but not terrifically helpful. Older children may be somewhat more reliable, but they may want to please the teacher or be particularly sensitive to the context—are they hungry, sad, or angry? No data was reported from student tests because the foundation made it clear that it didn't expect that sort of data. Although such data is easy to collect and compare, it's complicated to interpret.

We also gathered no classroom data on the preservice teachers. After all of this effort and resources, do they teach differently from their peers who traveled through the traditional program? We don't know. This would have been easier data to collect. Preservice teachers have no option about being observed; it is assumed they will be. We could have observed them and their peers to see if the project was successful. But we didn't.

The result is that there are large holes in the final evaluation. How did the MIE preservice students compare to others in the estimation of the student teaching supervisors? What did parents get out of their activities? Did student achievement change? These are major issues that escaped evaluation.

There is another reason to broaden the scope of an evaluation. The more lines of evidence available, the more certain the conclusions. It's dangerous to rely too heavily on any one source of data. For example, surveys are a good, quick way to get immediate feedback about a workshop or class. But the information can be unreliable in terms of classroom impact. Self-reports about change in teaching practice sometimes exaggerate the magnitude of change. But if we had access to classroom observations of change and our analysis confirmed our survey data, we could have more confidence in our conclusions. We got mountains of data, but it was from a limited range of sources.

Epilogue

I sit now in a university office. I am responsible for teaching pre-service teachers. Our department is entertaining a reinvention of our elementary education program. We will enter the brave new world of preservice cohorts, intensive experiences, increasing collaboration with the schools, and field-based courses cotaught by inservice teachers. Déjà vu all over.

I struggle about how to react to these initiatives. What advice would I give to my colleagues and those at other institutions about attempting a university–school collaboration? Can this epilogue inform other prologues? University–school collaborations are, despite any reservations I have, good ideas. It seems impossible to educate new teachers without them having contact with inservice teachers. New teachers need to be educated through attention to both university work and in-school work. If we think of other professions, medicine for example, classroom work makes sense. New physicians develop their clinical skills through supervised patient contact. And those who do the teaching have both a solid academic background and continuing clinical practice. We don't teach brain surgery without practice with real brains. Surgeons have done more than read good books on the subject. The same logic applies to another clinical practice—teaching. New teachers should be expected to demonstrate solid academic preparation coupled with real classroom teaching experience.

This doesn't sound avant-garde, but it is: It isn't commonly practiced in many teacher preparation programs. Why? Before a university and school enter preservice teacher matrimony, they need to address why and how the university and school systems have evolved the way they have. Before we can overcome some of these obstacles we have to understand them. Otherwise we can only treat symptoms.

Crossing the boundaries between universities and schools requires negotiation between different authorities. The schools and districts have their arenas of power and control. The universities have theirs. For a university and school to work together, everyone must know who has authority for what. We can choose to

101

accept these conditions and work together anyway but that might become cumbersome. In this circumstance, if I wanted to make a change I would have to work through two sets of conditions. The other option is to examine issues of authority and jointly decide to share authority. This sounds reasonable, but is more difficult than one would imagine. It is a challenge because both universities and schools are part of larger institutions that may not share the local decision to collaborate.

Although school systems and universities might point a finger at each other as being the problem in developing effective, thoughtful teacher preparation, my own bias is that universities are the more intractable. That may be heresy coming from a member of the club. The problems with coordination of universities and school systems to a common goal, taken as a whole, are huge. The university has a large set of interests, including research, scholarly writing, and securing external funding. Faculty must devote an enormous amount of energy to research, then they must write about it. These two activities can take up the bulk of faculty time. Projects like university–school collaborations require buckets of time. Such time isn't valued by the university unless it results in publishing articles. But where can the time to research and write about collaboration come from when the process itself is so time-consuming? The university is a big place with entrenched interests. A university–school collaboration will be small potatoes. It also will be viewed through an institutional lens. As in the classic story "Fish Is Fish" by Leo Lionni, the institution will try to make the unfamiliar more familiar by treating it like what already exists.

The university isn't out to undermine collaboration, but the major obligation and goal of the university isn't improving K–12 learning and teaching. That is a small component of a larger picture. The university would like all its projects to succeed, for public relations reasons if nothing else. But it keeps retreating to the familiar. For example, the supervision of student teachers is critical. But faculty have been removed from the process because it is time-consuming and expensive, so the collaboration ends at a critical point in the process. In other cases, innovative courses that cross departmental boundaries evaporate because of bureaucratic problems—who "owns" the course and where do the student credit hours go? If a university plans to engage in a collaboration with a school, it must be willing, and have the authority, to make major changes.

The schools also erect obstacles to university–school collaboration. Teachers have the ultimate weapon: to participate or not. A project won't go very far unless the teachers are invested in it. Teachers have to see value or the collaboration won't survive. It may be true, as others have suggested, that it is best if the schools and university "simultaneously renew" and commit to the collaboration, but I don't think it's absolutely necessary. If a university professor genuinely offers to help teachers teach better and humbly acknowledges that she has a lot to learn, many teachers would be willing to try. If we approach teachers by helping them improve student understanding, they will come along. They value that. They may not, at least initially, value their part in preservice education, but that can develop as the relationship between the university and school expands.

Funding collaboration efforts is often an issue. For a university–school collaboration to succeed, it must be part of the general budget. If grant money keeps it floating, it will dive when the grant expires. It may even be best if no seed money is used. If we have to pay people to try it, the commitment may be superficial.

As schools and universities start to collaborate, teachers and professors should come together as colearners for some part of the project. If university people are always giving workshops or leading study groups, the process of improving teaching becomes too traditional. The teachers still have the power to reject what the university faculty propose and the faculty can sit and talk about recalcitrant teachers. Nothing is changed. When can both sides come together and develop a common understanding of teaching?

Time is critical. Long-lasting institutional and cultural change takes time. Lots of it. It can barely begin in the time frame of most grants. There has to be a long-term commitment of both groups to staying the course. I believe we made some progress toward this outcome, but then the funding went away and LiC put a new cohort somewhere else in order to share the wealth. If you share the wealth too much, no one gets enough to make a difference. So other schools now benefit, temporarily, from LiC. In three years, the benefit will move on.

Finally, respect borders. Each institution has its own interests and values and does some things very well. I will never teach kindergarten; I'll leave that to others. I do a decent job preparing new teachers to teach science, though. I doubt many kindergarten teachers would want to trade. But university faculty and teachers can learn from each other. We may never move to "us" in terms of our roles and responsibilities. But what motivates us is knowing that we have a lot to learn and offer to each other. In the end, better teaching could be the reward of both schools and universities.

References

Barnett, C., D. Goldenstein, and B. Jackson. 1994. *Mathematics Teaching Cases: Fractions Decimals and Percents: Hard to Teach and Hard to Learn*. Portsmouth, NH: Heinemann.

House, P. 1994. "Implementing the Professional Standards for teaching mathematics: Let the mathematics-science connection break the mold in teacher preparation." *Mathematics Teacher, 87*(4), 289–93.

Hyde, A. A., M. Ormiston, and P. Hyde. 1994. "Building professional development into the culture of schools." In D. B. Aichele & A. F. Coxford (eds.). *Professional Development for Teachers of Mathematics,* 49–54. Reston, VA: NCTM.

Kennedy, M. M. 1998a. Form and substance in inservice teacher education. Research Monograph No. 13 Madison, WI: National Institute for Science Education.

———. 1998b. "Education Reform and Subject Knowledge." *Journal of Research in Science Teaching, 35*(3), 249–64.

Loucks-Horsley, S., P. Hewson, N. Love, and K. Stiles. 1998. *Designing Professional Development for Teachers of Science and Mathematics.* Thousand Oaks, CA: Corwin Press.

Ma, L. 1999. *Knowing and Teaching Elementary Mathematics.* Mahwah, NJ: Lawrence Erlbaum Associates.

National Council of Teachers of Mathematics. 1991. *Professional Standards for Teaching Mathematics.* Reston, VA: Author.

Nesbit, C., J. D. Wallace, D. Pugalee, A. C. Miller, and W. DiBiase. 2001. *Developing Teacher Leaders: Professional Development in Science and Mathematics.* Columbus, OH: ERIC.

Showalter, M. W. 1994. "Problems to Implement the NCTM's Professional Teaching Standards." *Mathematics Teacher, 87*(1), 5–7.

Weiss, J. 1990. Control in school organizations: Theoretical perspectives. In Clune, W. H. and Witte, J. F. (eds.), *Choice and Control in American Education, Volume 1: The Theory of Choice and Control in Education.* NY: Falmer Press.

Wiske, M. S. and C. Y. Levinson. 1993. "How Teachers Are Implementing the NCTM Standards." *Educational Leadership, 50*(8), 8–12.